KU-191-034

THE ASSOCIATION FOR SCOTTISH LITERARY STUDIES

NUMBER NINE

THE ASSOCIATION FOR SCOTTISH LITERARY STUDIES

ANNUAL VOLUMES PUBLISHED BY SCOTTISH ACADEMIC PRESS

1971 James Hogg. *The Three Perils of Man*. Ed. Douglas Gifford.

1972 John Davidson. *The Poems*. Vol. I. Ed. Andrew Turnbull.

1973 John Davidson. *The Poems*. Vol. II. Ed. Andrew Turnbull.

1974 Allan Ramsay and Robert Fergusson. *Poems*. Ed. Alexander M. Kinghorn and Alexander Law.

1975 John Galt. *The Member*. Ed. Ian A. Gordon.

1976 William Drummond of Hawthornden. *Poems and Prose*. Ed. Robert H. MacDonald.

1977 John G. Lockhart. *Peter's Letters to his Kinsfolk*. Ed. William Ruddick.

1978 John Galt. *Selected Short Stories*. Ed. Ian A. Gordon.

1979 Andrew Fletcher of Saltoun. *Selected Political Writings and Speeches*. Ed. David Daiches.

THE ASSOCIATION FOR SCOTTISH LITERARY STUDIES

GENERAL EDITOR — DAVID BUCHAN

ANDREW FLETCHER OF SALTOUN

SELECTED POLITICAL WRITINGS AND SPEECHES

EDITED BY

DAVID DAICHES

SCOTTISH ACADEMIC PRESS
EDINBURGH
1979

Published by
Scottish Academic Press Ltd
33 Montgomery Street, Edinburgh EH7 5JX

First published 1979
SBN 7073 0241 2

Introduction and Notes
© 1979 David Daiches

All rights reserved. No part of this publication may be
reproduced, stored in a retrieval system, or transmitted,
in any form or by any means, electronic, mechanical,
photocopying, recording or otherwise, without the
prior permission of Scottish Academic Press Ltd

Printed in Great Britain by
R. & R. Clark Ltd, Edinburgh

CONTENTS

ACKNOWLEDGEMENT

The Association for Scottish Literary Studies acknowledges the generous financial assistance of the Scottish Arts Council in the publication of this Volume.

INTRODUCTION

Andrew Fletcher of Saltoun (in East Lothian) was born in 1653, son of Sir Robert Fletcher of Saltoun and Innerpeffer and Catherine Bruce, daughter of Sir Henry Bruce of Clackmannan who claimed descent from the third son of King Robert Bruce's grandfather. His paternal grandfather, Andrew Saltoun, was one of the senators of the College of Justice in Scotland with the title of Lord Innerpeffer. His father died in 1665, having entrusted his son's education to Gilbert Burnet, the future Bishop of Salisbury and author of the *History of His Own Time*, whom as patron he had presented to the living of Saltoun earlier the same year. David Steuart Erskine, 11th Earl of Buchan, in a biography of Fletcher based on family papers which appeared in 1792, wrote: 'From Burnet he received, as might have been expected, a very pious and learned education, and was strongly imbued with erudition and the principles of a free government, which were congenial to the family of Fletcher, and espoused by his mother and by those who had, with her, the charge of his nurture.'[1] Burnet himself described Fletcher as 'a Scotch Gentleman of great parts and many virtues, but a most violent republican and extravagantly passionate', but in his unpublished manuscript he substituted for 'a most violent republican' the words 'a most passionate and indiscreet assertor of public liberty'.[2]

Burnet remained at Saltoun until 1669, when he was appointed Professor of Divinity at the University of Glasgow. G. W. T. Omond, in a biography of Fletcher published in 1897, suggests that Fletcher might have gone to Edinburgh University the year before Burnet left, for, he says, 'the name of an Andrew Fletcher occurs in the University of Edinburgh Register for the year 1668',[3] but subsequent examination of the Register has revealed no such name. Whether or not he attended Edinburgh University, we know that Fletcher completed his education by travelling abroad, though there is no record of the countries he visited. He may well have visited Holland, where he was to spend some time later and which already had both political and intellectual attractions for Scotsmen of Fletcher's cast of mind, and he probably also visited the countries that were on the itinerary of most young Scotsmen making the Grand Tour at this time – France, Germany, and Italy. On his return to Scotland he was sent as one of the members for Haddingtonshire or East Lothian to the Convention of Estates – a meeting of the estates of the realm held with less formality than a parliament – that met in June 1678.

At this time Scotland was being virtually ruled by the Duke of Lauderdale on behalf of his master Charles II. Charles had appointed Lauderdale Secretary of State for Scotland in 1661, and from 1667, when he succeeded the Earl of Rothes as Royal Commissioner for Scotland, until 1680, he ran the country. Lauderdale had worked hard, with royal support, in 1669 and 1670 to achieve a union of parliaments between Scotland and England, but the Scots still remembered the Cromwellian usurpation and successfully blocked the scheme, whose only immediate result was to strengthen the opposition to Lauderdale, who was already execrated by the Covenanters whom, having vainly attempted to win over to a moderate episcopalianism, he now proceeded against with increasing rigour. In 1678 he outraged the Covenanters of the south-west by quartering on them a body of 6,000 Highland and 3,000 Lowland troops, the so-called 'Highland Host'. Lauderdale expected a major rebellion and introduced repressive legislation to frustrate it (or, as Burnet thought, deliberately to force it). He also needed to raise money in order to maintain an army to put it down, and this was his main reason for summoning the Convention of Estates in June 1678.

The opposition to Lauderdale was led by the 3rd Duke of Hamilton, who in 1678 went to London with 'ten or twelve of the Nobility' and 'about fifty Gentlemen of quality' (Burnet) to lodge complaints against Lauderdale with the King. It was in their absence that Lauderdale summoned the Convention of Estates, confident that he could now manipulate it at will. 'And,' says Burnet, 'what by corrupting the Nobility, what by carrying elections, or at least disputes about them, which would be judged as the majority should happen to be at first, he hoped to carry his point. So he issued out the writs, while they were in London, knowing nothing of the design. And these being returnable in three weeks, he laid the matter so, that before they could get home, all the elections were over: And he was master of above four parts in five of the Assembly. So they granted an assessment for three years [it was in fact a land tax of £30,000 annually for five years], in order to the maintaining a greater force.'⁴ Fletcher watched the proceedings with indignation, and from now on became committed to a policy of no granting of taxation powers without prior guarantees of satisfactory government and also of bitter opposition to the maintaining of a standing army by the Crown. The Convention of Estates sat only from 26 June to 11 July: the opposition could muster only thirty-nine votes, including Fletcher's, while the Government obtained one hundred.

Something of Fletcher's habit of mind is revealed by a story of his behaviour during this short session told by his contemporary Lord Fountainhall. The Estates had ordered that only members should be admitted to Parliament House, but Fletcher's brother Henry managed to get in, only to be discovered, fined, and sent to the Tolbooth. The next day Fletcher 'pitched on little William Tolemache as no member' and Lauderdale had to point out formally that Tolemache was one of his servants and therefore he was entitled to come with Lauderdale into the House before the matter was resolved.[5]

Lauderdale's policy was now to turn the militia in Scotland into a standing army equipped to put down rebellion. Accordingly, the Scottish Privy Council was ordered to call out 5,000 foot and 500 horse from the militia and quarter them throughout the counties of Scotland at the expense of the landed proprietors. The soldiers were ordered not only to swear the oaths of allegiance and supremacy but also, individually, to swear to maintain the established order in Church and State and to oppose the 'damnable principle' of taking arms against the King or his representative. Two hundred foot and forty-six horse from this 'New Model' (as this army came to be called, in Cromwellian phrase) were quartered upon Haddingtonshire, to Fletcher's indignation. Lord Fountainhall records that on 29 July 1680 'at Privy Council, Fletcher of Saltoun, Sinclair of Stevenston, and Murray of Blackbarronie are pannelled for seditiously and factiously opposing, at least obstructing, his Majesty's service, in putting the Act of Privy Council to executions for levying the 5500 men out of the militia'. Though it was thought that they would be fined or imprisoned, they were unexpectedly let off with a 'rebuke'. In January 1681 'the Lord Yester, Salton, and the other gentlemen of East Lothian' petitioned the Privy Council complaining of the standing forces and their quartering upon them. This petition, says Fountainhall, 'was extremely resented, because it called quartering contrary to law, and seemed to derogate from the King's prerogative, and reflected on the Government'.[6]

In the election of 1681 Fletcher and Adam Cockburn of Ormiston were returned for Haddingtonshire by freeholders opposed to the

Government. Their opponents were the Government supporters Hepburn of Humbie and Wedderburn of Gosford, and they claimed to have been rightfully elected. The matter was referred to the Committee on Disputed Elections, where the Bishop of Edinburgh, John Paterson (a man treated by Burnet in the most contemptuous terms as a servile creature of the Court) proposed that 'for the sake of serving the King' some of the votes given to Fletcher should not be counted. But this was not done, and Fletcher and Cockburn were declared duly elected. By this time Lauderdale's reign in Scotland had ended: he was recalled in 1680, after the destruction of the Covenanting army at Bothwell Brig on 22 June by a royal army with troops from England under the Duke of Monmouth, one of several events which were taken to indicate the ineffectiveness of Lauderdale's policy. He was replaced as High Commissioner in Scotland by Charles II's brother, the Duke of York, and it was he who summoned the Scots Parliament on his arrival in Scotland in 1681, triumphant in his brother's successful manœuvring to stop the English Parliament from passing an Exclusion Bill to prevent him, as a Roman Catholic, from succeeding to the throne. His first object now was to secure his succession to the Scottish throne also, and he managed to get the Scots Parliament to pass an Act asserting that no religious difference could prevent the lineal heir from succeeding. Parliament then went on to pass an 'Act anent Religion and the Test', in the debate on which Fletcher played a conspicuous part.

Fletcher spoke in opposition to the Test Act, then decided to move that the security of the Protestant religion should be made one of its objects, a motion that the Government (or Court Party, as contemporaries called it) could hardly oppose. The result, however, was an extraordinarily confused piece of legislation. The test was to be taken by every person holding public office, down to schoolmasters and clerks on the civil side and members of the rank and file on the military side. Those taking the test had to 'own and sincerely profess the true Protestant religion contained in the Confession of Faith received in the first Parliament of King James the Sixth, and . . . believe the same to be founded on and agreeable to the written Word of God'. They also had to 'disown and renounce all such practices, whether Popish or fanatic, which are contrary to or inconsistent with the said Protestant religion and Confession of Faith'. At the same time they had to affirm their belief 'that the king's majesty is the only supreme governor of this realm over all persons and in all causes as well ecclesiastical as civil'. When Fletcher proposed to make the security of the Protestant religion

x

one of the objects of the Test Act, he cannot have wanted this; indeed, he cannot have wanted to do anything other than embarrass the Government, which in a sense is what he did. For, taken together with the preceding Act of Succession, the Test Act showed a fundamental inconsistency; the person whom the Act of Succession had confirmed as heir to the throne and who would soon become 'the only supreme governor of this realm over all persons and in all causes as well ecclesiastical as civil', was himself a Papist. The Test Act professed to renounce equally Roman Catholicism and Covenanting Protestantism – in favour of the old Knoxian Confession of Faith, 'a book', says Burnet, 'so worn out of use, that scarce anyone in the whole Parliament had ever read it'. The 9th Earl of Argyll, of whom the Duke of York was deeply suspicious as the powerful son of a Covenanter and supporter of the Cromwellian administration in Scotland who had been executed after the Restoration, when called upon to take the test, said, according to Burnet, that 'he did not think that the Parliament did intend an oath that should have any contradictions in one part of it to another; therefore he took the test as it was [that is, in so far as it was] consistent with itself'.[7] The Duke of York insisted on Argyll's being brought to trial for treason, and he was tried and condemned to death. Though he escaped abroad, he was executed later on the same charge after returning to Scotland in support of Monmouth's rebellion against James after the latter's accession to the throne in 1685.

Fletcher had by now drawn upon himself the implacable enmity of the Duke of York. Though not a man of passionate religious (as distinct from moral) beliefs, he was passionate in his opposition to anything that smacked of arbitrary power in either Church or State. As one of the Commissioners of Supply for Haddingtonshire, he had the duty of arranging for the troops quartered on the county: in April 1682 he and some other Commissioners were accused by the Lord Advocate before the Privy Council of not meeting with the Sheriff-Depute to set prices on corn and straw, grass and hay, for the soldiers' horses or at least for making a mock of the task by not taking it seriously. There is no doubt that Fletcher did all he could to thwart the Government in its most cherished objectives. It soon became clear to Fletcher that for his own safety he had better leave Scotland, and in 1683 he and Robert Baillie of Jerviswood, in the Earl of Buchan's words, 'came into England in order to concert measures with the friends of freedom in that country; and they, I believe, were the only Scotchmen who were admitted into the secrets of Lord Russell's Council of Six. They were likewise the only persons in whom the Earl of Argyll confided in Holland the common measures of the two countries, which were then concerned with much secrecy and danger, for the recovery of the constitution and liberties of the British kingdoms.'[8]

The Council of Six were a group who managed the affairs of English dissidents who were opposed to the policies of Charles and his brother. They included Charles's illegitimate son the Duke of Monmouth, Richard Hampden, who had moved the Exclusion Bill in 1679, the Earl of Essex, who was soon to be sent to the Tower for his anti-Government plotting and was found with his throat cut out in July 1683, Lord Howard, who had earlier suffered imprisonment for his plotting, Lord Grey, who was to command Monmouth's horse at the battle of Sedgemoor in 1685 and survived by giving evidence against his associates, and Lord Russell, who was soon to be executed for high treason after being convicted of complicity in the Rye House plot. We do not know exactly what part Fletcher took in anti-Government plottings in England, though it is certain that neither he nor Baillie of Jerviswood had anything whatever to do with the Rye House plot. This did not prevent the Government from arresting and, after a hideous mockery of a trial, sentencing and executing Jerviswood for alleged complicity in the plot. He was offered his pardon if he would implicate his friend Fletcher but, in Lord Buchan's words, 'he persisted to the gallows in rejecting the proposal with indignation'.[9] After the discovery of the Rye House plot neither England nor Scotland was a safe place for a known enemy of the Government and associate of anti-Government malcontents, and later in 1683 Fletcher went abroad. He was reported in Paris in October of that year, and soon afterwards we find him in Holland, the natural refuge for both Scottish and English opponents of the royal brothers. The Earl of Argyll was there, and Monmouth, and many others, discussing what might happen and what they should do on the death of Charles II. When Charles died in 1685 and his brother succeeded him as James VII of Scotland and II of England, the prospect of England and Scotland in the hands of a Papist royal absolutist led to thoughts of new action, while on James's side the presence of Monmouth in Holland aroused his suspicion and he tried to persuade the Prince of Orange (who was his son-in-law) to expel him. Eventually, in April 1685, against Fletcher's advice, Argyll left to raise a rebellion in Scotland having exacted a promise from Monmouth that he would set sail to provide co-ordinated action in England within six days. Monmouth fulfilled his obligation, though later than the agreed date. Bad weather

xii

delayed the start of the expedition until the end of May. Fletcher, who disapproved of Monmouth's expedition as he disapproved of Argyll's as he was sceptical of their success, nevertheless sailed with Monmouth, for he considered that, having made his decision, Monmouth ought to be supported.

Monmouth intended Fletcher to be joint commander of his horse, but as it turned out Fletcher never fought in the fatal battle of Sedgemoor that was eventually to cost Monmouth and so many of his supporters their lives. What Burnet calls 'an unhappy accident' forced Monmouth to dismiss Fletcher from his service. Burnet explains: 'He sent him out on another party: And he, not being yet furnished with a horse, took the horse of one [Heywood Dare, Mayor of Taunton] who had brought in a great body of men from Taunton. He was not in the way: So Fletcher, not seeing him to ask his leave, thought that all things were to be in common among them, that could advance the service. After Fletcher had rid about, as he was ordered, as he returned, the owner of the horse rode on, who was a rough and ill-bred man, reproached him in very injurious terms, for taking out his horse without his leave. Fletcher bore this longer than could have been expected from one of his impetuous temper. But the other persisted in giving him foul language, and offered a switch or a cane: Upon which he discharged his pistol at him and fatally shot him dead. He went and gave the Duke of Monmouth an account of this, who saw it was impossible to keep him longer about him, without disgusting and losing the country people, who were coming in a body to demand justice. So he advised him to go aboard the ship, and to sail on to Spain, whither she was bound. By this means he was preserved for that time.'[10] So on 13 June Fletcher left England on the *Helderenberg* for Bilbao. The Earl of Buchan says in his biographical sketch that Fletcher later in life told George Keith, the Earl Marischal, that he left Monmouth because the latter had, contrary to his promise, proclaimed himself King. But Monmouth proclaimed himself King at Taunton on 20 June, a week after Fletcher left the country, so this cannot be true. It was the 'Dare incident', eloquent of Fletcher's proud character and hasty temper, that forced him to leave the country and so saved him from the fatal consequences of Monmouth's defeat at Sedgemoor.

Fletcher's adventures in Spain were recorded by George Keith, 10th Earl Marischal, the exiled Jacobite who became Frederick the Great's ambassador in Paris in 1751, governor of Neufchatel in 1752, and in 1758 ambassador in Madrid. The Earl Marischal was born about 1693, and when he set down many years later what Fletcher had told him about his Spanish adventures he must have been recalling a conversation that occurred when he (the Earl Marischal) was a very young man (Fletcher died in 1716, when the Earl Marischal was little past twenty). According to this account, Fletcher was committed to prison soon after his landing in Spain and on the application of the English Minister at Madrid was ordered to be delivered up and transmitted to London in a specifically designated Spanish ship. However, Fletcher was rescued from prison by a mysterious stranger and then proceeded to move throughout Spain in disguise, buying 'many rare and curious books', before leaving the country to fight as a volunteer against the Turks in Hungary. The details of this are obscure, as are also the details of his move to Holland, where he eventually joined other English and Scottish expatriates looking to the prospect of an invasion of England by William of Orange.

Fletcher had been in trouble at home almost from the moment he left for England with Baillie of Jerviswood in 1683. In November 1684 he was cited 'at the market-cross of Edinburgh and pier and shore of Leith' to answer the charge of 'conversing with Argyle and other rebels abroad' and the following January was cited with other 'fugitive rebels who were abroad' to appear before Parliament on 26 March to be tried for treason. However, before his execution Argyll had cleared Fletcher of plotting with him by testifying that he had written several times to Fletcher without getting a reply, so that charge was dropped. But the main charge against Fletcher was that he had participated in Monmouth's rebellion, that he 'rode up and down the country with him, and was in great esteem with him for two or three days; and continued in open rebellion with him till, having killed one Dare, an English goldsmith, who was likewise with him in the said rebellion, he was forced to fly in the frigates in which they came and make his escape'.[11] The trial came on in the High Court of Justiciary on 21 December 1685, the prosecutor being the Lord Advocate, Sir George Mackenzie ('Bluidy Mackenzie'). On 4 January 1686 Fletcher was found guilty and condemned as a traitor to lose both his life and his estates and to suffer all the indignities the law of treason inflicted on the person, the family, and the descendants of an attainted traitor. His estates were granted to the Earl of Dumbarton, a brother of the Duke of Hamilton whom he appointed to manage them for him.

Fletcher, safely in Holland, joined William of Orange at the Hague in 1688. In November 1688 he sailed with William for Torbay and from there returned to Scotland. James VII fled abroad and William accepted the invitation of a group of English magnates to take the throne of England jointly with his wife (who was James's daughter). The English Parliament proclaimed William and Mary joint sovereigns of England in February 1689. In Scotland the Convention of Estates met at Edinburgh on 14 March to decide whether to follow the example of the English Parliament and offer William and Mary the throne of Scotland. A pro-William President, the Duke of Hamilton, was chosen by a small majority; John Graham of Claverhouse, Viscount Dundee, leader of the Jacobite (pro-James) party, rode off in disgust to raise a Jacobite army in the Highlands. The Convention, freed from pressure from Claverhouse and his group of Jacobite horse, finally proclaimed on 11 April 1689 that King James VII had forfeited the Crown of Scotland ('being a profest Papist' and having 'by advice of Evil and Wicked Counsellors invaded the Fundamental Constitution of the Kingdom, and altered it from a Legal, limited Monarchy, to an Arbitrair and Despotick Power') and declared William and Mary King and Queen of Scotland. The declaration included a 'Claim of Right' asserting the nation's 'ancient Rights and Liberties' and declaring among other things that 'no Papist can be King or Queen of this Realm', that 'all Proclamations asserting an absolute Power' in matters of religion were contrary to law, as were 'the imposing of Oaths without Authority of Parliament', imprisonment without trial, the enforcing of 'old and obsolete Laws upon frivolous and weak Pretences', the use of torture in trials and the quartering of troops in private houses. It also asserted that 'Prelacy and the Superiority of any Office in the Church, above Presbyters, is, and hath been a great and insupportable Grievance and Trouble in this Nation, and contrary to the Inclinations of the Generality of the People, ever since the Reformation . . . and therefore ought to be abolished'. The Claim of Right also asserted the right of subjects to petition the King, and asked for frequent parliaments 'and the Freedom of Speech and Debate secured to the Members'. The Convention also set out 'Articles of Grievances' repudiating the whole machinery of government set up since the Restoration and much of the legislation enacted.

Fletcher, to his indignation, was not a member of this Convention of Estates, but he followed its proceedings with passionate interest. He was much concerned with the Claim of Right and its clause 'against a Popish king' (as he wrote to Sir Patrick Hume on 18 September 1689): this was not out of religious prejudice, for Fletcher was easy on religious matters, but because of his fear, based on his experience of James VII's government, that a Roman Catholic king would mean royal absolutism. Though Fletcher supported William, whose displacement of James made his own return to Scotland possible, he was by nature a political independent and did not automatically support William's policy or the Court Party which sought to implement it. In fact, he became a member of an opposition political group in Edinburgh called 'The Club', which at first consisted both of Whigs disappointed of office under William and of Scottish patriots worried about the preservation of Scottish rights and privileges (Fletcher came in the second category); it later had dealings with Jacobites also.

Fletcher was watching carefully the situation in England as well as in Scotland. In January 1689, optimistic about the chances of the English Parliament imposing on the new King the kind of limitations on royal power that he always favoured, he supported a union between England and Scotland: 'We can never come to any trew setelment but by uniting with England in Parliaments and Trade' he wrote in a letter of 8 January. He changed his mind on this point in the light of subsequent events. His Scottish nationalism was always a means to specific ends – the dignity, political freedom, and economic prosperity of the people of Scotland – and these ends could be achieved in a variety of ways. It was only when he saw proposals for an 'incorporating union' between England and Scotland as likely to lead to the frustration rather than the achievement of these ends – and it was a series of events beginning with the damaging English hostility to the Company of Scotland Trading to Africa and the Indies and England's part in the disastrous ending of the Scots settlement in Darien that led him to this view – that he became a passionate opponent of such a union.

The union of Scotland and England, supported by Fletcher in 1689, was recommended by William in a letter he sent to the Convention in Edinburgh in March of that year: 'We are glad to find, that so many of the Nobility and Gentry, when here at London, were so much inclined to an Union of both Kingdoms, and that they did look upon it as one of the best Means for procuring the Happiness of these Nations, and settling of a lasting Peace amongst them, which would be advantagious to both, . . .'[12] On 23 April the Convention passed an Act nominating eight persons from each of the three estates (the peers, the county members – known as the barons – and the borough members) 'to treat concerning the Union of the two Kingdoms'. But at this stage there was no interest in a Union in England, and the Act was never implemented. The real interest of those Scotsmen who were anxious to use the acceptance of William as King as a means of improving Scotland's position was in the conditions to be attached to such an acceptance – conditions which were set out in the Claim of Right. Ever since the Union of the Crowns in 1603 Scotland had been managed by royal appointees in the interests of a Court policy framed by the King's English advisers: the Cromwellian interlude was of course an exception to this, but the forced Cromwellian union of the kingdoms was not an acceptable precedent to any party at this time. How to make sure that if Scotland shared a king with England the true interests of the northern kingdom would not be sacrificed to those of her southern neighbour and the dignity and welfare of Scotland would be pursued by a Scottish Parliament free to determine its own policy – this became increasingly the main concern of Scotsmen like Fletcher. As William increasingly showed that his interest in Scotland was essentially confined to getting Scottish help in what was essentially his private war against France, and as his approval (however passive) of the Massacre of Glencoe in 1692 and his acceptance of English sabotaging of the Company of Scotland in 1695–8 (having originally approved the Act setting it up) showed how little his concern for Scotland was, Fletcher became increasingly disillusioned with the man whose accession to the throne of both England and Scotland he had at first supported. Most Scotsmen engaged in politics at this time acted in their own interests and played their own hand. The most powerful members of the Scottish nobility, the 'magnates', exploited the need of the English Court to 'manage' Scotland in their own interests by playing the system for all it was worth and making what they could out of it. Fletcher was one of the few who acted consistently out of principle rather than out of private interest. John Hamilton, 2nd Baron Belhaven, and George Baillie of Jerviswood were two others who showed similar independence of mind: the three of them made some of the most interesting speeches about the constitutional position of Scotland in the fierce debates on Union that went on in Scotland's last Parliament between 1703 and 1707.

The officers sent down from Scotland to administer the oath to William and Mary did not insist on any prior conditions, nor did they require that the new King and Queen subscribe to the Claim of Right: they simply presented the Claim of Right and the Articles of Grievances to William for him to read at leisure and presumably for him to act on or not as he thought fit. It soon became clear, to Fletcher at least, that William was not in fact to be hedged in by the sort of conditions that would prevent royal policy riding roughshod over Scotland's interests, so that even before Glencoe and Darien he was growing increasingly suspicious of the new monarch. He joined 'The Club', as we have seen. The passionately anti-Union Jacobite, George Lockhart of Carnwath, who wrote an account of Scottish affairs from Queen Anne's accession to the Union of 1707, greatly admired Fletcher's stand, though Fletcher was neither a Roman Catholic nor a Jacobite, and even if his account of his attitude is somewhat over-simplified it does give a genuine contemporary view of what Fletcher was about:

> Andrew Fletcher, of Salton, in the first part of his Life, did improve himself to a great Degree by Reading and Travelling; He was always a great Admirer of both Ancient and Modern Republicks, and therefore the more displeas'd at some Steps which he thought Wrong in King Charles the Second's Reign, whereby he drew upon himself the Enmity of the Ministers of that Government, to avoid evil Consequences of which, he went abroad; during which Time, his Enemies Malice still continuing, he was upon slight frivolous Pretences, Summon'd to appear before the Privy Councul, and their Designs to Ruin him being too apparent, he was so enrag'd, that he concurred, and came over with the Duke of Monmouth, when he Invaded England; upon which he was Forfeited. Thereafter he came over with the Prince of Orange; But that Prince was not many Months in England, till he saw his Designs, and left him, and ever thereafter hated and appeared as much against him, as any in the Kingdom.[13]

Fletcher's suspicion of William did not prevent him from supporting the Government when a counter-revolution threatened in 1692. When the Duke of Hamilton was superseded as High Commissioner for Scotland by the Earl of Melville, and showed his displeasure by sulking in his tent, it was Fletcher who wrote to him to lay aside his personal grievances and assist the Government in the face of a threat of a French invasion. As the Earl of Buchan put it: 'When an attempt was made in 1692 to bring about a counter-revolution, Fletcher's ruling principle (though dissatisfied with King William) was the good of his country. He used all his influence with the Duke of Hamilton to forget the causes of his disgust, and to co-operate with the friends of a free constitution.'[14] Hamilton, whether as a result of Fletcher's persuasion or not, did return to public life, and after the French-Jacobite threat was removed by the victory of the English fleet at La Hogue he remained active. He became Royal Commissioner again in 1693 and died the following year.

During William's reign the political conflicts in Scotland centred on the differences between the Court Party and the Country Party, the former representing English interests and the latter resenting English interference. Fletcher was associated with the Country Party (which, like The Club, attracted both Whig and Tory dissidents), although he always remained his own man and throughout his political career was essentially an independent. Lord Buchan, who contrasted Fletcher's disinterested devotion to 'the interest and honour of Scotland', with the attitude of those who sought power or emoluments for themselves, tells an interesting story to illustrate his views on monarchy: 'Being in company with the witty Dr. Pitcairn, the conversation turned on a person of learning whose history was not distinctly known. "I knew the man well," said Fletcher: "he was hereditary professor of divinity at Hamburgh." "*Hereditary* professor!" said Pitcairn with a laugh of astonishment and derision. "Yes, Doctor," replied Fletcher, "hereditary professor of divinity. What think you of a hereditary king?" '[15]

On 5 June 1689 the Meeting of Estates passed an Act declaring itself to be 'a Lawful and Free Parliament' and it sat intermittently until the summer of 1702, when William died. On 30 June 1690, after protests by Fletcher at the delay, Parliament passed an Act restoring him his estates and former privileges. The abolition in 1690 of the Lords of the Articles, a committee of Parliament controlled by the Crown so as to ensure royal influence on motions and decisions, meant that from now until its abolition in 1707 the Scots Parliament was an independent forum of discussion and decision-making to a degree that it had never been before. Fletcher was not at this time a member, but he must certainly have supported the decision to abolish this committee. He took a keen interest in the arguments that were going on inside and outside Parliament about the economic state of the country and the powers of the monarchy in Scotland. Fletcher appears to have been influential in bringing William Paterson's plan for a trading settlement in Darien to the attention of the authorities in Scotland and he continued active in promoting the scheme and in voicing his concern and indignation at its failure. His twin concern with the nature of royal power and with the economic plight of Scotland is shown in his earliest published writings, *A Discourse Concerning Militias and Standing Armies* published in London in 1697 and again in Edinburgh in 1698 as *A Discourse of Government with relation to Militias* (modified so as to concentrate on the Scottish implications, whereas the first edition was addressed to English readers and took its examples from English history), and *Two Discourses Concerning the Affairs of Scotland, Written in the Year 1698*, published in Edinburgh in 1698. It is the Scottish version of the *Discourse Concerning Militias* that is included in this selection of his works.

The *Discourse Concerning Militias* argues that it was the superseding of the old feudal method of recruiting into the King's army by means of the barons calling out their vassals by a 'standing mercenary army kept up [by the royal government] in time of peace', the unintended but inevitable result of a variety of developments in the Renaissance, that brought the menace of standing armies to Europe 'to her affliction and ruin'. The whole question of standing armies was then being vigorously debated in England, and Fletcher's essay was a contribution to a central seventeenth-century controversy. He drew on a variety of historical examples to make his point that 'mercenary armies [are] exactly calculated to enslave a nation' and went on to argue that the country could best defend itself 'by well-regulated militias against any foreign force, though never so formidable'. His specific proposals for such a militia involved the setting up of four camps, one in Scotland and three in England 'in which all the young men of the respective countries should enter, on the first day of the two and twentieth year of their age; and remain there the space of two years, if they be of fortunes sufficient to maintain themselves; but if they are not, then to remain a year only, at the expense of the public'. He proceeds to put forward a very Spartan régime for those serving in the militia. The camp would be 'as great a school of virtue as of military discipline'. The virtues to be inculcated were 'modesty, obedience, patience in suffering, temperance, diligence, address, invention, judgement, temper, [and] valour'. Fletcher's harsh idealism emerges strongly in his insistence that in the camp 'punishments should be much more rigorous than those inflicted by the law of the land' and that there should be punishment for some things that the law of the land allows. 'No woman should be suffered to come within the camp, and the crimes of abusing their own bodies any manner of way, punished with death.' The whole scheme is presented in considerable detail as a practicable way of dealing with the defence of the country by means of an army of temporarily conscripted young citizens instead of by a mercenary standing army. The combination of precise and detailed plans combined with a highly theoretical and sometimes quite unrealistic view of the practicalities of human nature was characteristic of Fletcher.

The first of Fletcher's *Two Discourses Concerning the Affairs of Scotland* is concerned with trade and politics. He deplores Scotland's backwardness in trade: '. . . partly through our own fault, and partly by the removal of our kings into another country, this nation, of all those who possess good ports, and lie conveniently for trade and fishing, has been the only part of Europe which did not apply itself to commerce; and possessing barren country, in less than an age we are sunk to so low a condition as to be despised of all our neighbours, . . .' As always when Fletcher analyses a defect in Scottish life, it is attributed to a change brought about by the Union of the Crowns or by royal policy since then, and contrasted with an often idealized situation before then. He stresses the importance of the African and Indian Company and deplores the 'undermining' of this and other Scottish enterprises by English pressures and the underhand dealings ('though without his majesty's knowledge as we ought to believe') that resulted in withdrawal of English capital. He refers particularly to 'the affair of Hamburgh'. When the Scots were prevented by the Dutch from raising money for their company in Amsterdam, since the Dutch had their own East India trade to protect, they tried Hamburg, but the English Resident, Sir Paul Rycaut, egged on by English merchants, successfully prevented the Scottish company from raising money there. Rycaut's behaviour leads Fletcher to assert that Scotland should have separate ministers representing the country abroad, not only in matters of trade 'but upon all occasions, wherein the honour or interest of the nation is concerned'. He points out that ever since Scotland had the same king as England, both countries had only a single minister where representation abroad was required, and this was because the minister was a representative of the King: but in fact he represented the interests of the larger and richer country, England, rather than those of the smaller and poorer. This is but one of many illustrations brought forward by Fletcher throughout his writings and speeches of the evils wrought to Scotland by having the same king as England without guarantees that protected Scottish interests. At the same time Fletcher believed, and states in this essay as elsewhere, that it is misunderstanding that leads people to believe that one country's economic prosperity depends on its keeping another country down: properly understood, he argues, the economic interests of Holland, England, and Scotland are compatible and the prosperity of one should encourage the prosperity of all.

Fletcher goes on to argue that 'in place of laying a land tax upon the kingdom for maintaining forces to defend the English and Dutch trade, we should raise one for the carrying on of our own'. Scotland is exhausted of money by 'a three years' scarcity next to a famine' (the 'dearth of monies' was to be a continuing problem for Scotland for some years) and had lost many of her people who had served either as seamen or as soldiers for King William in 'a long and tedious war' which 'is at length ended in peace' (the War of the League of Augsburg, concluded by the Treaty of Ryswick, 1697). Consideration of Scottish losses in the war leads him back to the question of a standing army versus a militia. He reminds his readers that 'the keeping up of a standing army in time of peace, without consent of parliament [was] an article of forfaulture of the late king James'. (The Articles of Grievances had included this clause: 'That the Levying, or keeping on Foot a standing Army in Time of Peace, without Consent of Parliament, is a Grievance.') He goes on to give both economic and moral arguments against standing armies, then proceeds to discuss the proper relations between King and Parliament and to object to a land tax being granted to the King for life. He concludes, somewhat surprisingly, with a plea for conspicuous punishment for Jacobite supporters of the counter-revolution who had insinuated themselves back into office and would therefore be likely 'to betray his present majesty into the same misfortunes that were brought upon the late king'. At the same time, he protests that the guilty men in the Massacre of Glencoe were never punished. An Act of Indemnity is only healing and beneficial after 'the greatest offenders are punished', and he argues that Parliament 'should proceed, without delay, to the punishing of the greatest criminals, both of this and the last reign'. Fletcher was not a vindictive man, and in the debate on Union in Scotland's last Parliament he could co-operate with Jacobites in patriotic manœuvres and he certainly aroused the admiration of some of them. But where any question of the revival of royal absolutism arose, or of those in the pay of an English Court pursuing policies detrimental to Scotland, he was unyielding in his enmity.

Fletcher's *Second Discourse Concerning the Affairs of Scotland* is concerned entirely with Scotland's economic plight. As we have seen, he was not at this time a Member of Parliament, but he was writing to advise Parliament what it should do. 'The first thing that I humbly and earnestly propose to that honourable court, is, that they would take into their consideration the condition of so many thousands of our people who are, at this day, dying for want of bread.' When Fletcher was writing Scotland was in the midst of what became known as the 'seven ill years' of failed harvests and famine. The harvests failed to meet the needs of the country in 1695 and 1696; in 1697, although the weather was less appalling and a reasonable harvest could be expected, the shortage of seed corn resulting from the previous year's bad harvest limited the amount produced; 1698 and 1699 were again bad years, and bad harvests with consequent widespread poverty and starvation went on until 1703. (The biblical seven years were really eight.) Henry Gray Graham has given a classic account, compiled from contemporary sources, of this period: 'During these disastrous times the crops were blighted by easterly "haars" or mists, by sunless, drenching summers, by storms, and by early bitter frosts and late snow in autumn. For seven years this calamitous weather continued – the corn rarely ripening, and the green, withered grain being shorn in December amidst pouring rain or pelting snow-storms. Even in the months of January and February, in some districts many of the starving people were still trying to reap the remains of their ruined crops of oats, blighted by the frosts, and perished from weakness, cold and hunger. The sheep and oxen died in thousands, the prices of everything among a peasantry that had nothing went up to famine pitch, and a large proportion of the population in rural districts was destroyed by disease and want.'[16] 'We do not know', comments a modern historian, Rosalind Mitchison, 'how many starved and died, but the accounts show us the full horror of the old-fashioned famine, sustained so long that the very young, the old, and the weak, who might have got through a single bad year, could not hope to last out. "Everyone may see Death in the Face of the Poor," wrote Sir Robert Sibbald. Families begged, people died of hunger in the streets, and the epidemics that followed shortage finished off still more.'[17]

The severity of the crisis explains the tone of Fletcher's pamphlet and the desperate nature (as most of us today would consider it) of his remedy – the restoration of a controlled and humane slavery which would at least guarantee food, shelter, and clothing to the enslaved. He is well aware of the shock his proposals would give to most of his readers. 'Would I bring back slavery into the world? Shall men of immortal souls, and by nature equal to any, be sold as beasts? . . . But they must pardon me if I tell them, that I regard not names, but things.'

The system he proposes – and we must be careful to note the qualifications and conditions he insists on – would bring to many people, Fletcher argues, a better life than men of all ranks lead under arbitrary government. But the main advantages he sees in his scheme are economic rather than political. In spite of the carefully argued historical precedents and the insistence on regarding actual practical consequences rather than general theories about freedom, there is a note of desperation, almost of hysteria, in Fletcher's discussion. Even his figures, which he must have made up, for there were no reliable statistics then available, suggest this. His estimate that 'there are at this day in Scotland . . . two hundred thousand people begging from door to door', which he considers double the number in normal times, is not a real figure but a symptom of his acute anxiety. His concern with the blatantly immoral life of the masses of roving vagabonds who preyed on the country also lies behind his proposals. Controlled servitude is better than vagabondage. Fletcher considers that the causes of the present poverty and misery in Scotland lie largely in the land renting system, which he proposes to change drastically.

The pamphlet was an honest if in some respects a desperate attempt to remedy a desperate situation, and it is worth noting that Ramsay MacDonald, who wrote an admiring article on Fletcher in 1893, saw his proposals as radical rather than reactionary. But Fletcher himself was not really hopeful that they would be accepted. 'I know that these proposals, by some men who aim at nothing but private interest, will be looked upon as visionary: it is enough for me, that in themselves, and with regard to the nature of the things, they are practicable; but if, on account of the indisposition of such men to receive them, they be thought impracticable, it is not to be accounted strange: . . .' His solution may have been freakish, but it was a sincere and wholly disinterested attempt to solve the appalling economic and social problems then facing Scotland.

Fletcher's next published work – anonymous, like all the others – was written in Italian and entitled *Discorso delle cose di Spagna Scritto nel mese di Luglio 1698*. It bears the imprint 'Napoli 1698' but was actually printed in Edinburgh. It first appeared in English translation in the 1749 Glasgow edition of Fletcher's *Political Works*. It deals with the power position in Europe resulting from the emergence of the Spanish succession question and in particular from the First Partition Treaty of 1698. It is a curiously ironical and convoluted argument professing to show how indirectly, and without anybody (apparently) except Fletcher noticing it, a course of events might be embarked on that would lead to Spain's attainment of world empire. It is not included in this present selection, as of less interest to the modern reader than most of Fletcher's other works, and certainly of less interest to those mainly concerned with Fletcher's involvement with Scottish affairs. A similar air of ironic knowingness (not characteristic of Fletcher's other writings) colours his *Speech upon the State of the Nation*, which does not seem ever to have been actually delivered as a speech nor to have been published in Fletcher's lifetime. The only known copy is in the Bodleian Library, Oxford: this has a pencil note under the title-heading 'in April 1701, by Fletcher'. It was probably published after 1704, and it is included, as are the other works of Fletcher mentioned, in the *Political Works* of 1732 and 1739. The speech shows, in a remarkable round-about way, how King William might be planning to make himself an absolute monarch of an empire that included Britain and the Low Countries. It is not included in the present selection as, like the pamphlet on Spanish affairs, of little general interest today.

Fletcher sat once more for East Lothian in the Scottish Parliament which opened at Edinburgh in May 1703. William had died the previous year (his wife Mary having died childless in 1694); in England the Declaration of Right had settled the crown on Mary's sister Anne. In Scotland the Claim of Right had similarly designated Anne as heir to the throne if Mary failed to produce offspring. But Scotland did not go as far as England did in the English Parliament's Act of Settlement of 1701, which settled the Crown of England on Sophia, Electress of Hanover, and her descendants. Sophia was a granddaughter of James VI and I. It was her son, George, Elector of Hanover, who eventually succeeded on Queen Anne's death in 1714. But a momentous debate was to take place before that succession was assured in Scotland, and Fletcher played a leading part in it.

The fact that the Scottish Parliament left open the question of the succession to the Scottish throne after Queen Anne's death was a constant source of irritation and apprehension to English politicians, who saw Scotland as a back door by which a French-assisted Jacobite attempt to restore the Stewarts could be made. The more they pondered the problem the more they saw what appeared to be the absolute necessity of Scotland's continuing to share the same monarch as England. And eventually it appeared that the only effective way to ensure this was to achieve an 'incorporating union' between Scotland and England, eliminating the Scottish Parliament and giving paramount authority throughout Britain to the Westminster Parliament which would inevitably have a permanent minority of Scottish members. Thus the primary motive for English support of an incorporating union was political: economic and even ecclesiastical English interests tended to be against union. In Scotland, on the other hand, the only truly persuasive arguments for union were economic. Those who were against union in Scotland feared not only for the dignity and independence of Scotland but also feared the increased probability that Scotland would after the union be governed even more than in the past in the interests of what was known as the English Court, i.e., English politicians out for their own ends.

On Anne's succession in 1702 the same Parliament that had brought William to the throne of Scotland was reassembled by Anne and her ministers because it seemed favourable to union and to the unconditional granting of supplies. But its legality was questioned: after the death of a monarch a new election should have been called and a new Parliament elected. The 4th Duke of Hamilton who, though he had fought for King James against Monmouth, was now chief parliamentary spokesman for Scottish national feeling, demanded the dissolution of this Parliament and new elections. In this he was joined by members of the Country Party, who were largely Presbyterians whose Scottish national feeling had been outraged by events in William's reign but who also included some Jacobites. Hamilton led these members out of the House in protest against the lack of new elections and in their absence the Commissioner, the 2nd Duke of Queensberry, a man relied on by the Court Party, was able to get the remaining 120 members to pass an Act for the appointment of Commissioners to treat for a Union of the two Kingdoms of Scotland and England. Two sets of Commissioners were appointed, one from each country, but they could not agree on Scots demands about trade and soon reached deadlock. It was clear that a new Scottish Parliament, whose legality was beyond doubt, would have to be elected. This was done, and Fletcher, as we have seen, once more represented his native county.

The 1703 parliamentary elections in Scotland showed three main parties in conflict: the Court Party, representing the English Government and the Queen's ministers; the Country Party, also known as the Patriotic Party, led by the Duke of Hamilton and supported by Fletcher; and the Jacobites, who agreed with the Country Party in demanding free trade with England and a policy for Scotland freed from English interests but differed from them in looking to young James (son of the exiled James VII, who had died in 1701) as the rightful heir to the throne of both countries. Many of the Jacobites were Episcopalians, but often less committed to their religious position than the Whig Presbyterians.

On the advice of Sir George Mackenzie of Tarbat, who had been appointed joint Secretary for Scotland with Queensberry on Anne's accession and who on 1 January 1703 was created Earl of Cromarty and Viscount of Tarbat, the Queen leaned towards the Tories during and immediately after the 1703 elections and even wooed the Jacobites, who were assured by the Earl of Seafield, now Lord Chancellor (roughly the equivalent of Speaker of the House), that if they recognized Queen Anne and supported the Government against the Country Party they would be tolerated as Episcopalians and allowed to have a share in the conduct of affairs, and an indemnity was issued for all acts of treason since the Revolution. The Jacobites responded favourably to this overture by calling themselves Cavaliers. Queensberry was again Commissioner. George Lockhart of Carnwath, in his *Memoirs of the Affairs of Scotland, from Queen Anne's Accession . . . to the Commencement of the Union of the Two Kingdoms . . .*, gives a Jacobite view of the parliamentary situation in 1703:

> At the time when the Parliament met there were different Parties or Clubs, First, the Court Party, and these were Subdivided into such as were Revolutioners, and of Antimonarchichal Principles, and such as were any thing that would procure, or secure them in their Employments and Pensions, and these were directed by the Court in all their Measures. Secondly, The Country Party, which consisted of some (tho' but few) Cavaliers, and of Presbyterians, of which the Duke of Hamilton and the Marquis of Tweeddale were Leaders. Thirdly, the Cavaliers, who, from the House they met in, were call'd Mitchel's Club, of whom the Earl of Home was the Chief Man.[18]

At the time of the opening of the new Parliament there was considerable argument going on in Scotland about the conditions under which the successor of Queen Anne to the Scottish throne should be invited. Almost simultaneously with its opening, the Whig journalist George Ridpath published anonymously *An Historical Account of the antient Rights and Power of the Parliament of Scotland* arguing, somewhat unhistorically, that traditionally Scotland's monarchy had always been limited by the ultimate sovereignty of Parliament and offering the work 'to the consideration of the Estates when they come to settle limitations for the next successor'. These 'limitations' were the great argument among Scottish patriots and a positive obsession with Fletcher. The objective was to find ways of limiting the royal power in order to prevent that power, and the power of the monarch's English advisers, from being used in English rather than Scottish interests. It is interesting that the Cavaliers, who wanted the return of the Stewarts who had been exiled largely for the absolute way in which James VII had asserted the royal prerogative, joined the Country Party in supporting these limitations drawn together by a common nationalism.

After the ceremonial opening of Parliament on 6 May 1703 – the last time the old feudal ceremony of 'riding the Parliament' was to take place – the Government were confident that, in view of their concessions to Tory feeling and to the Jacobites and the diminished numbers of the Country Party who were returned to Parliament, they would have a majority in support of their policies, which were to settle the Scottish succession in the same way as it had been settled in England, to raise revenue to pay for the Government forces in Scotland, and to achieve an incorporating union between Scotland and England to close permanently the back door into England and to dispose once and for all of the possibility that Scotland might choose a monarch different from England. On 19 May the Earl of Home, by previous arrangement with Queensberry (in the words of David Hume of Crossrigg's invaluable diary of the events in this Parliament) 'gave in a motion by way of Act, for a supply, all blank in the sum and time'. But instead of this being carried immediately, as Queensberry and his men hoped, the Marquis of Tweeddale, representing the Country Party, produced a motion that before any other business 'the Parliament might proceed to make such conditions of government and regulations in the Constitution of this Kingdom to take place after the decease of Her Majestie and the heirs of her body as shall be necessary for the preservation of our religion and liberty'. Queensberry, desperate for an Act of Supply without which the Government could not be run, tried to persuade the Country Party that if they voted for an Act of Supply plenty of time would be afforded later for discussion of religion and liberty. Hume of Crossrigg records that in answer to this 'it was said they might very much rely upon the Commissioner's word, but what if contrary orders should come from

Court, it was known the Treasurer of England behoved to be consulted on our affairs before the Queen were acquainted'.[19] The Duke of Hamilton praised the Treasurer of England as 'a very worthy person' but added that though he would give no ill advice to the Queen 'still Englishmen will give advice with regard to their own country'. Fletcher then joined the debate, asserting that an Act of Supply should be the final rather than the initial Act of any session of Parliament, or at least it should 'lie upon the table, till all other great Affairs of the Nation be finish'd, and then only granted'. This is the first of Fletcher's 1703 parliamentary speeches, which were printed in Edinburgh the same year as *Speeches by a Member of Parliament which Began at Edinburgh the 6th of May, 1703* and which were reprinted in the 1732 London *Political Works* and the 1749 Glasgow *Political Works*. They are the most important of all Fletcher's political speeches and are printed in this selection exactly as they appear in the original editions except for somewhat more modern spelling and punctuation.

'I move, therefore,' Fletcher's speech concluded, 'that the house would take into consideration what acts are necessary to secure our religion, liberty and trade, in case of [Queen Anne's death], before any act of supply, or other business whatever be brought into deliberation.' The motion provoked what Hume of Crossrigg called 'long, and tedious, and nauseous repetitions in debate, till candles were brought in',[20] after which the proceedings were adjourned until two days later, 28 May. The Cavaliers had now reconsidered their favourable response to the Government's overtures and were moving towards a coalition with the Country Party in a concerted attempt to assert the national interest. Government supporters tried to drive wedges between the two parties especially between Presbyterians in the Country Party and Episcopalians in the Cavalier Party, by introducing divisive ecclesiastical questions, but they had no success in this and the Commissioner, seeing that the combined votes of the members of the two parties would prevail, gave way gracefully and accepted without a vote Fletcher's motion 'that Parliament will proceed to make such Acts as are necessary for securing our Religion, Liberty, and Trade, before any Act of Supply, or any other Business whatever'.

Members of the Country Party, Cavaliers, and Jacobites regarded the passing of this motion as a triumph. Lockhart of Carnwath recorded:

Then the Parliament proceeded to frame and finish such
Acts as tended to secure their liberties and Freedom from the

Oppression they sustained thro' the Influence of English Ministers over Scots Counsels and Affairs, in which a long time was spent, many bold Speeches, and excellent Overtures being made, the Court strenuously opposing them all; and the Cavaliers, and Country Party, as strenuously Insisting, at last prevailed, and carried in Parliament these Two valuable Acts; First, An Act anent Peace and War; Declaring, among other Things, That after Her Majesty's Death, and failing Heirs of Her Body, no Person, at the same Time King or Queen of Scotland, and England, shall have sole power of Making War with any Prince, State, or Potentate whatsoever, without consent of Parliament: . . . And, Secondly, that Excellent and Wisely contriv'd Act of Security, which has since made such a Noise in Britain.[21]

The debates on the Act of Security, which occupied Parliament from 9 June to 13 August, were extremely fierce. Sir John Clerk of Penicuik, member for Whithorn, wrote in his *Memoirs*: 'At times we were often in the form of a Polish diet with our swords in our hands, or, at least, our hands on our swords.' On 9 June Lord Belhaven, as Hume of Crossrigg recorded, 'had a long discourse on the attempts of Union with England, both before K. James 6, and since, and the kingdom's encroachments ever since, and their endeavours to exalt the prerogative here, to sett up Episcopacy to enthral us, not on a religious account: he was by some desired to print his discourse'.[22]

On 22 June 1703 Hume of Crossrigg recorded in his diary: 'Given in by the Marq. of Montrose, a Draught of an Act for security of the kingdom; two by the Ld. Advocate, a long one and a short one to the same purpose; one by Salton [Fletcher] containing 12 limitations upon the successor. After long altercation, Agreed these four should be allowed to be printed by the Sollicitor, and given to the Members of Parliament, against next Sederunt.'[23] George Ridpath's anonymous account of the proceedings of this session of Parliament, published in 1704, says 'that which was most taken notice of and came nearest to the Act that the House agreed to, was the draught given by Mr. Fletcher of Salton'.[24] Fletcher's draught for an Act of Security, which includes his famous twelve limitations, is one of his important political statements and his speeches in favour of it go to the roots of his political thought. Earnest and eloquent though he was in pleading for his limitations, Fletcher was unable to convince a majority of the House of their necessity, but a considerable amount of their substance was included in the Act of Security which, after weeks of fierce debate in which the Act was discussed clause by clause, was finally hammered out and approved by about sixty votes, with many abstentions.

The Act of Security, after specifying how and where Parliament should meet after Queen Anne's death and providing for various contingencies, went on to authorize and empower the Estates of Parliament 'to Nominate and Declare the Successor to the Imperial Crown of this Realm, and to settle the Succession hereof upon the Heirs of the said Successor's Body, the said Successor, and the Heirs of the Successor's Body, being always of the royal LINE of Scotland, and of the true Protestant religion'. Then came the crunch: 'Providing always, That the same be not Successor to the Crown of England, unless that in this present Session of Parliament, or any other Session of this or any ensuing Parliament during her Majesty's Reign, there be such Conditions of Government settled and enacted, as may secure the Honour and Sovereignty of this Crown and Kingdom; the Freedom, Frequency, and Power of Parliaments, the Religion, Liberty, and Trade of the Nation from English or any Foreign Influence; with Power to the said Meeting of Estates, to add such further Conditions of Government as they shall think necessary, the same being consistent with, and nowise derogatory from those which shall be enacted in this, and any other Session of Parliament during her Majesty's Reign . . . And it is hereby expressly provided and declared, That it shall be high Treason for any person or persons to administer the Coronation Oath, or be Witnesses to the Administration thereof, but by the Appointment of the Estates of Parliament in manner above mentioned, or to own or acknowledge any Person as King or Queen of this Realm in the Event of Her Majesty's Decease, leaving Heirs of her own Body, until they have sworn the Coronation Oath in Terms of the Claim of Right: And in the Event of Her Majesty's Decease, without Heirs of her Body, until they Swear the Coronation Oath, and accept on the terms of the Claim of Right, and of such other Conditions of Government, as shall be settled in this, or any ensuing Parliament, or added in the said Meeting of Estates, and be thereupon declared and admitted as above; which Crime shall be irremissible without Consent of Parliament.'[25]

On 16 July the Earl of Roxburgh ('a Man of good Sense', wrote Lockhart of Carnwath, 'improven by so much Reading and Learning, That, perhaps, he was the best Accomplish'd Young Man of Quality in Europe, and had so Charming a way of expressing his Thoughts, that he pleased even those 'gainst whom he spoke')[26] moved the vital clause preventing the successor to the Crown of England from also being the successor to the Crown of Scotland unless Scotland's conditions had been met. It contained the essence of Fletcher's limitations and produced furious debate before Fletcher moved that it should be voted on. Seafield, the Chancellor, then declared it was late and Queensberry, the Commissioner, adjourned the session until the next morning. 'Then there was a great cry and hubbub,' reported Hume of Crossrigg, 'the Privilege of Parliament and the Claim of Right was encroached upon; and the D. of Hamilton, the E. of Rothes, Marquis of Tweddale, &c., took a Protest thereon, and many adhered, and said they would address the Queen; . . . but afterwards, on second thoughts, when the Commissioner was come out they came out, and went to Pat. Steil's.'[27] (Patrick Steil was the keeper of the Cross Keys tavern and was known for his musical interests and concerts.) The next morning the Chancellor tried to soothe offended members by explaining that it was simply the late hour, not any desire to encroach upon the privileges of the House, that motivated his adjournment. But Fletcher insisted that the adjournment had been illegal. There was a long discussion, and eventually the high feeling abated and the question of the legality of the adjournment was not voted on.

Seafield and Queensberry now tried to replace Roxburgh's dangerous clause with a less dangerous one, which simply said that Scotland should not have the same King or Queen as England 'unless there be a Communication of trade with England agreed to, Freedom of navigation, and Trading with their plantations, &c., as shall be satisfying at the sight of the Parliament of Scotland'. Fletcher spoiled this ploy by accepting the new motion (put up by Sir James Stewart, the Lord Advocate) and then moving that *both* clauses, this one and Roxburgh's, should be put to the vote together. The Lord Advocate intervened to start a diversion by raising a question about seating in the House, and discussion of this occupied the rest of the day. On 23 July Roxburgh moved both clauses, and the Lord Advocate had to accept this, but added to Roxburgh's clause the words, 'unless there be such conditions of government made in this or any other Session of this or any other Parliament during the Queen's reign, or in the Meeting of Estates'. Hot debate followed on which clause should be voted on or whether they should be voted on together. Finally on 26 July a conflated version of the two clauses was passed by seventy-two votes.

Seafield and Queensberry knew that this would give displeasure to their London masters. Seafield wrote placatingly to Sidney Godolphin, Lord Treasurer of England, explaining and justifying his manœuvre of adjourning the House on the evening of 16 July. He wrote again after the vote of the 26th, emphasizing the strength of the opposition. If Parliament insists on refusing to pass an Act of Supply 'there will be great difficultie to preaeserve authoritie and government', yet they made approval of such an Act conditional on the kind of guarantees demanded by the offending clauses.[28] Godolphin in London was in no mood for compromise: he disliked equally both the clause introduced by the Lord Advocate as a substitute for Roxburgh's and Roxburgh's original clause. His main object was to prevent any legislation by a Scottish Parliament that would, under any conditions whatever, prevent the succession to the throne in Scotland from being different from that in England. So he instructed Queensberry not to 'touch' the Act of Settlement – touching it with the ceremonial sceptre was the sign of royal approval and necessary for an Act to come into force. The resentment shown by Scottish patriots was extremely fierce, and Fletcher spoke with both passion and reason on the subject. The excitement of the debate is vividly captured by Lockhart of Carnwath's description:

'Tis needless and would be endless to repeat, suppose I could, the Discourses that were made *Pro* and *Con*, whilst the Parliament was upon Overtures to secure their Liberties, and redeem the Nation from the Oppression it groaned under: 'Tis sufficient to say, That the Court opposed every Thing that could be proposed for that End, and, in Return, were so baffled in all their Schemes and Designs, That when a Motion was made for Granting a first Reading to the Act for a Supply, the Parliament flew in the Face of it, some Demanding the Royal Assent to the Act of Security, others asking, If the Parliament met for nothing else than to drain the Nation of Money, to support those that were Betraying and Enslaving it? And after many hours warm Debates on all Sides, a Vote was stated, *Whether to proceed to Overtures for Liberty, or a Subsidy?* And the House being crowded with a vast Number of People, nothing, for near Two Hours, could be heard but Voices of Members, and others (it being late, and Candles lighted) requiring Liberty and no Subsidy.[29]

The state of the debate and the attitude of Queensberry at different points in it can be easily seen from the nature of Fletcher's interventions. Eventually, when all his eloquence and persuasiveness had no effect in persuading Queensberry to touch the Act of Security, he decided on 15 September that 'it will be highly necessary to provide some new laws for securing our liberty upon the expiration of the present intail of the crown' – and so he returned to the question of limitations, concentrating on the first and most important. No progress was made on either side. On 16 September the frustrated Queensberry asked the Chancellor to adjourn Parliament until 12 October. It did not in fact meet again until 6 July 1704. The Act of Security had not received the royal assent.

Though he had not succeeded in getting his limitations passed or in persuading the Commissioner to touch the Act of Security, Fletcher had the satisfaction of seeing the House pass in September an 'Act anent Peace and War' that embodied one of his limitations; it enacted that after Queen Anne's death without heirs of her body, no King or Queen of Scotland could declare war without consent of the Scottish Parliament and that any declaration of war without such consent should not be binding on the subjects of 'this Kingdom'. Oddly, perhaps, this Act did receive the royal assent, in the hope 'to have obtained a subsidy for the Army'. The hope was in vain.

The 1703 session was a notable session of the Scottish Parliament, in which Fletcher played a notable part. Lockhart of Carnwath understandably regarded it as the most glorious of all sessions of the Scottish Parliament:

> And thus I have thro' this Session of Parliament, which did more for Redressing the Grievances, and Restoring the Liberties of this Nation, than all the Parliaments since the 1660 Year of God: And it cannot be thought strange, that Scots-men's Blood did boil to see the English (our inveterate enemies) have such influence over all our Affairs, that the Royal Assent should be granted or refused to the Laws the Parliament made, as they thought proper; and, in short, every Thing concerning Scots Affairs determined by them, with regard only to the Interest of England; To see Bribing and Bullying of Members, unseasonable Adjournments, and innumerable other Ungentlemanny Methods made use of, to seduce and debauch People from the Fidelity they owed to that which ought to be dearest to them, I mean the Interest, Welfare, and Liberty of their Country and Fellow-Subjects, by whom they were entrusted in that Office.

These Considerations, I say, enraged and embolden'd a great Number of Members to such a Degree, that many strange and unprecedented Speeches were made, Enveighing against, and Exposing the Government, especially by that worthy and never to be enough praised Patriot Andrew Fletcher, of Salton.[30]

The Government, frustrated at not getting the desperately needed finance by means of an Act of Supply, tried to make good the deficiency by introducing an Act allowing the importation of 'Wines and other Foreign Liquors' from abroad, which meant in fact that wine could be freely imported that came ultimately from France with which the country was officially at war. This Act was the last passed by the 1703 session of Parliament, in spite of the fierce opposition of both the Cavaliers and the Country Party. (It is significant that the Cavaliers, with their Jacobite proclivities, who might have been thought to favour France where the exiled Jacobite Court was, were against this Act: it shows how strongly they felt about denying the Government further sources of revenue until Scottish national demands were met.) Fletcher made two strong speeches against the Act.

In December 1703, with Parliament in recess, Fletcher had leisure to write an important political work, *An Account of a Conversation Concerning the Right Regulation of Governments for the common good of mankind in A Letter to the Marquis of Montrose, the Earls of Rothes, Roxburgh, and Haddington*. It was published in Edinburgh in 1704 and was included in both the London and the Glasgow *Political Works*. In form this work is a Platonic dialogue, purporting to be, and undoubtedly based on, an account of a conversation on politics he had recently had in London with the Earl of Cromarty, Sir Edward Seymour, and Sir Christopher Musgrave. It sets Fletcher's views clearly in the context of conflicting views about Anglo-Scottish relationships and about government generally, and goes on to develop a highly original theory of devolution for the British Isles which in some respects sounds surprisingly modern.

The new session of Parliament opened on 6 July 1704, with the Marquis of Tweeddale now Commissioner. Three leading members of the Country Party had had an audience with the Queen in February and impressed her by their reasonableness. As a consequence, the Country Party accepted office in support of the Hanoverian succession and Queensberry was replaced by Tweeddale. The Earl of Cromarty remained as sole Secretary for Scotland and Sir James Murray, a Queensberry supporter, was replaced as Lord Register by James Johnston, who had been Godolphin's chief adviser on Scottish affairs and through whose mediation agreement between the Court and the Country Party had been achieved.

The Government now hoped that they could move quickly to settle the succession question in the way they wanted, but they were disconcerted when, on 11 July after the opening official speeches appealing for unity throughout Britain, William Seton of Pitmedden, junior, moved that while the House would stand by and defend Her Majesty's person and government without naming a successor to the crown of Scotland, during the present session of Parliament, it would nevertheless 'agree on such Conditions of Government to take Effect after her Majesty's Death, as might best conduce to free that Kingdom from all English Influence, to the end the Scots might be in a Condition to Treat with England, about a Federal Union' (a federal union was distinguished from an incorporating union: the former was seen by many supporters of union in Scotland as the only kind of union that would be in Scotland's national interest and the latter was seen as a sinking of Scottish identity and interests in the English). On 13 July the Duke of Hamilton proposed 'That this Parliament will not proceed to the Nomination of a Successor, untill we have had a previous treaty with England, in relation to our commerce, and other concerns with that Nation.' Fletcher supported Hamilton's proposal. According to Lockhart, he 'elegantly and pathetically set forth the Hardships and Miseries to which we have been exposed, since the Union of the two Crowns of Scotland and England in one and the same Sovereign; and the Impossibility of amending and bettering our Condition, if we did not take Care to prevent any Design, that tended to continue the same, without other Terms, and better Security than we have hitherto had'.[31] The Government countered with a compromise resolution aimed both at placating Scottish national feeling and securing the nomination of a successor to the Crown, but Hamilton out-manœuvred them by accepting this resolution and proposing that it be taken jointly with his own. It was carried by forty-two votes that the vote should be one on the combined resolutions, which the Cavaliers saw as an assertion of Scottish rights, and, with the solid support of the Cavaliers, the joint measure was then passed by a majority of fifty-five. This was popularly taken as a great triumph for the cause of Scottish freedom from English domination.

On 25 July the Duke of Hamilton once again moved the reading of the Act of Security, but this time added it as a clause to the Act of Supply, making it quite clear to the Government that he was seeking a *quid pro quo*. This so-called 'tacking' of one Act to another was regarded in Government circles as, in the Lord Clerk Register's words, 'a straitening of the Queen, who might possibly consent to the one, and not to the other'. Hume of Crossrigg described the debate that ensued and Fletcher's part in it:

> Salton said, He knew, and could make it appear, that the
> Register had undertaken to prosecute the English designs for
> promotion to himself. Reg. said, There could be no Influence
> but the Place he had, and it was known he had lost a higher
> place for his concern for his country. Some called, That Salton
> should go to the bar for accusing a Member. Salton, backed by
> D. Hamil. said, The Letter by the Queen to the Parliament was
> written when no Scotsman was about her, and so behoved to
> be by English influence. The Reg. said, It came up to the
> Queen from Scotland; that he believed there was no English
> man would be at the pains to draw a letter. Salton still insist-
> ing, Sr. Ja. Hacket said, He was impertinent. Salton said, He
> that would call him Impertinent was a Rascal. The House
> being alarmed at such expressions, S. J. Ersk moved Both
> should be sent to prison. The Chancel. gave a sharp rebuke to
> both; and it resolved in this, first Sr. Ja. Halket then Salton,
> Declared they were sorry they said any thing that had given
> offence to the House, and promised upon their word of
> honour, they should not take any notice of it else where.[32]

With the army in Scotland unpaid and the threat of a Jacobite rising with French assistance always in the background, the Government were desperate for money. After further insistence by members of Parliament that no action on supply should be taken until the Queen had given her assent to the Act of Security, Tweeddale, totally nonplussed, consulted his masters in London and was finally instructed to 'touch' the Act of Security. So on 5 August 1704 the Act of Security was again read and voted, and this time it received formal royal approval. The House then proceeded at once to pass by a unanimous vote an Act granting supply for six months.

This did not put an end to fierce debate in the House. Arguments about a lack of official inquiry into the so-called Scots Plot, arguments in which Fletcher was involved with others, accusations (made by Fletcher) that the House of Lords were meddling in Scottish affairs and consequent accusations and counter-accusations resulted in some bitter exchanges. The Government could find no way of mitigating the anti-English implications of the Act of Security, and the 1704 session of Parliament, during which the Government had hoped for a successful compromise, ended in a mood of defiant confrontation between the two countries. The Scots Parliament passed an Act prohibiting the importing of woollen cloth from England and allowing the exporting of wool and yarn in competition with that of England. The session concluded on 28 August with the passing of a remonstrance to the Queen deploring the misbehaviour of the House of Lords and the lack of inquiry into the Scots Plot. On 5 February 1705, when the Scots Parliament was in recess, the English House of Commons passed and sent to the Lords the Alien Act, providing that after 25 December 1705 Scotsmen in England should be treated as aliens and English exports to Scotland and imports to England should virtually cease. It set the deadline almost a year ahead in order to give the Scots time to respond to the blackmail and work for 'a nearer and more complete Union' with England. On 14 March the Alien Act received the royal assent.

The next session of the Scottish Parliament opened on 28 June 1705. The young Duke of Argyll was now Commissioner, Queensberry was Lord Privy Seal, Argyll's relative, the 3rd Earl of Loudoun, a strong advocate of Union, was joint Secretary for Scotland with the Marquis of Annandale. Seafield remained Chancellor. The parties were now the Court Party, supporting the Government, consisting mostly of Whig Ministers; the Country Party, which now called itself the New Party; and the largely Jacobite and Episcopalian Cavaliers. The New Party, now independent of both the Cavaliers and the Court, included (and were sometimes regarded as identical with) a group widely known as the 'Squadrone Volante', opportunist in tactics, nationalist in feeling, and formally supporting the Hanoverian succession with limitations. Fletcher worked with the Squadrone, though he always remained his own man.

The Government were now more than ever committed to an incorporating union as the only solution to the problem of the succession and the threat posed by the Act of Security. The Marquis of Lothian, an active unionist, presented a draft of an Act of Union. Fletcher put forward a resolution that 'notwithstanding the unneighbourly and injurious useage receaved by ane act lately past in the Parliament of England' the Scottish Parliament were still willing 'in order to a good understanding between the two nations' to enter into a treaty with England, but that it was inconsistent with the honour and interest of 'this independent kingdome to make any act or appoint Commissioners for that same end' until the English Parliament had made such a proposal 'in a more neighbourly and friendly manner'. Arguments about limitations were followed by arguments about trade. Parliament proceeded to pass a number of Acts safeguarding the Scottish position after the Queen's death but none of these received the royal assent. Fletcher returned to his Limitations. In a long discourse he 'set forth', says Lockhart, 'the deplorable State to which the Nation was reduced, by being subjected to English Councils and Ministers, while one and the same Person was King of both Kingdoms' and 'presented a Scheme of Limitations, which he proposed should be ingrossed into an Act'.[33] These were the same as his original twelve limitations, but this time he wanted them to be adopted by Claim of Right rather than by Act of Parliament. The Government violently rejected this on the grounds, as Seafield wrote to Godolphin on 18 August, that it was tantamount to setting up a republic after the Queen's death. The Earl of Mar's motion for a Treaty of Union which provided that the appointment of officers of state should be subject to the consent of Parliament, first offered on 20 July, came up again on 25 August and gave members an opportunity to voice their indignation at the Alien Act. 'Salton, Belhaven, and in the end, the Dukes of Ham. and Athol spoke against Treating till the injurious Act of Parliament in England were rescinded', Hume recorded.[34] Fletcher 'represented the scurrilous and haughty Procedure of the English in this Affair; and exhorted them to resent this Treatment, as became Scotsmen, by throwing the Motion of a Treaty, until it were proposed in more civil and equal Terms, out of the House with Indignation'.[35] Fletcher's motion was rejected. Hamilton proposed the addition of a clause to Mar's draft treaty that 'the Union to be treated on, should no Ways derogate from any fundamental Laws, ancient Privileges, Offices, Rights, Liberties, and Dignities of this Nation'. Fierce argument ensued, with the Court Party strongly opposing the clause and others arguing, often both subtly and passionately, that the clause did not imply a mistrust of the Queen herself since 'she was not in a Capacity to know the Interest and Circumstances of Scotland, so well as that of England'. Eloquent statements were made about the Scots being 'a free, independent people' with power to give whatever instructions they pleased to the Commissioners. Hamilton's clause was finally rejected.

On 28 August Fletcher returned to his argument about removing the affront to Scotland's honour and dignity before any proposal for a treaty of Union could be favourably considered, and he put forward the draft of an address to the Queen:

> We your Majesties most Loyal and Faithful Subjects, the Noblemen, Barons and Burgesses concerned in Parliament, humbly represent to your Majesty, That the Act lately past in the Parliament of England, containing a Proposal for a Treaty of Union of the two Kingdoms, is made in such injurious Terms to the Honour and Interest of this Nation, that we who represent this Kingdom in Parliament, can no ways comply with it, which we have the greater regret to refuse, because a Treaty of Union has in this Session been recommended to us by your Majesty; but out of the Sense of the Duty we owe your Majesty, we do declare that we shall be always ready to comply with any such Proposal from the Parliament of England, whenever it shall be made in such terms as are no ways Dishonourable and Disadvantageous to the Nation.

On 3 September Seafield reported to Godolphin that they could only make progress with legislation for Union if the Alien Act was revoked. While not actually promising directly to do this, the Government compromised by agreeing that a resolution that the Alien Act should be rescinded should be presented as an address to the Queen. This had the intended effect. On 1 September 1705 the draft Act for a Treaty of Union was read and approved and further, on a motion, surprisingly by Hamilton himself, it was carried that the Scottish Commissioners for Union should be nominated by the Queen rather than by Parliament, thus ensuring that the Commissioners would support an incorporating rather than a federal union. Fletcher was among the most bitter of those who protested, but to no avail. An incorporating Union between Scotland and England was now a certainty, and the debates and wrangles that went on after the Commissioners had formulated and presented their proposals for Union and they were debated clause by clause, though often rising to a high pitch of eloquence, were really little more than shadow boxing. Between 3 October 1706, when Scotland's last Parliament met in its final session, and 16 January 1707 when the Act to approve the Articles of Union was read for the second time and passed by 109 votes to 69 (with Fletcher among the thirty 'barons' who voted against it) the Government kept up every kind of pressure, both political and financial, to ensure that waverers voted their way. Throughout the discussion of each clause Fletcher intervened when he could, though his speeches were never published and we must go to Hume of Crossrigg and Lockhart of Carnwath for some indication of what he said. There is a story said to have originated with Lord Elibank, that after the passing of the Treaty of Union, as Fletcher was leaving Edinburgh in despair, he was anxiously asked, 'Will you forsake your country?' to which he replied, 'It is only fit for the slaves who sold it.'[36]

Fletcher was not against a union between Scotland and England, but he supported a federal and opposed an incorporating union. His proposals for a federal union were put forward in his last published work, *State of the Controversy Between United and Separate Parliaments*, which appeared in 1706. Here he argued that a proper union between the two countries should allow for separate parliaments, for with Scots as a permanent minority in a Parliament where the English will always have a vast majority there would be no way to prevent Scottish interests from being sacrified to English. He is scornful of the notion that all would now be 'British', making fun of 'this dream of being one and not two' and pointing out that in any case the British Parliament would consist mostly of English, and even if they asserted that they were legislating for the benefit of Britain it would be for their own benefit, for they too would now be British. He has no use either for the proposals that sixteen representative Scottish peers should sit in the House of Lords. 'It is plain that in process of time, an united Parliament would mumble this spurious race of Scots into nothing, for very obvious reasons.'

In 1708 Fletcher was one of those opponents of Union suspected of being involved in an abortive French invasion in the interests of the Jacobite Pretender James Francis Edward. He was arrested and sent to Stirling Castle, where he seems to have been well treated. There was no real evidence against him, and he was eventually set at liberty. He now retired from public life and devoted himself to farming and agricultural improvement in which he played a conspicuous part. He died in 1716.

The dominant part that Fletcher played in Scotland's last Parliament might suggest that he was a natural orator. But he was not; he confessed himself to have no facility in impromptu speaking and had to write out and memorize all his speeches. He is described in a manuscript quoted in the 1749 Glasgow edition of his *Political Works* as 'a low, thin man, of a brown complexion; full of fire; with a stern, sour look'. Lockhart of Carnwath, a fellow patriot and opponent of an incorporating union though differing strongly from Fletcher in many matters, paid most eloquent tribute to him: 'He was a Learned, Gallant, Honest, and every other way well Accomplish'd Gentleman, and if ever a Man proposes to serve and merit well of his Country let him place his Courage, Zeal, and a Constancy as a Pattern before him, and think himself sufficiently applauded and rewarded, if he obtain'd the Character of being like Andrew Fletcher, of Salton.'

Fletcher never married, saying on one occasion that his brother got the wife that he had wanted. He was irascible, hot-tempered and in some respects intolerant. His passionate idealism could sometimes result in quite unrealistic and even cruel proposals. But all his life he acted for what he considered the good of the people of Scotland, never seeking office or any other benefit for himself.

A full account of the political context within which Fletcher's pamphlets and speeches were produced will be found in the present writer's *Scotland and the Union* (London, 1977).

The text of the pamphlets and speeches here reprinted is taken from *The Political Works of Andrew Fletcher, Esq.*, London, 1732. This reprints accurately the original pamphlets but with a somewhat more modern spelling and punctuation. The Glasgow edition of 1749 is also an accurate reprint but modernizes spelling and punctuation rather more. The present text is therefore in the tradition of continuous discreet modernising combined with otherwise accurate reprinting, and it is hoped that it will be accessible to a wider reading public than a simple reproduction of the original pamphlets.

1. *Essays on the Lives and Writings of Fletcher of Saltoun and the Poet Thomson: Biographical, Critical, and Political*, by D. S. [David Steuart] Earl of Buchan, London, 1792, p. 5.
2. *History of His Own Time*, by Gilbert Burnet, London, 1725, Vol. III, p. 1046.
3. *Fletcher of Saltoun*, by G. W. T. Omond, Edinburgh and London [1897], p. 12.
4. Burnet, *op. cit.*, Vol. II, pp. 742–3.
5. Omond, *op. cit.*, p. 14.

6. *Ibid.*, p. 16.

7. Burnet, *op. cit.*, Vol. II, p. 901.

8. Buchan, *op. cit.*, p. 9.

9. *Ibid.*, p. 10.

10. Burnet, *op. cit.*, Vol. III, pp. 1065–6.

11. *Andrew Fletcher of Saltoun, His Life and Times,* by W. C. Mackenzie, Edinburgh, 1935, p. 329, footnote 3, cites the relevant sources.

12. *Acts and Orders of the Meeting of the Estates of the Kingdom of Scotland, holden and begun at Edinburgh, March 14, 1689,* Edinburgh, 1731, p. 144.

13. *Memoirs Concerning the Affairs of Scotland from Queen Anne's Accession to the Commencement of the Union of the Two Kingdoms of Scotland and England in May, 1707* [by George Lockhart of Carnwath], London, 1714, pp. 68–9.

14. Buchan, *op. cit.*

15. *Ibid.*, pp. 37–8.

16. *The Social Life of Scotland in the Eighteenth Century,* by Henry Grey Graham, Edinburgh, 1899, Vol. I, p. 146.

17. *A History of Scotland,* by Rosalind Mitchison, London, 1970, p. 292.

18. Lockhart, *op. cit.*, p. 35.

19. *A Diary of the Proceedings in the Parliament and Privy Council of Scotland May 21 MDCCC.–March 7, MDCCVII.,* by Sir David Hume of Crossrigg, Edinburgh, 1828, p. 100.

20. *Ibid.*, p. 101.

21. Lockhart of Carnwath, *op. cit.*, p. 55.

22. Hume of Crossrigg, *op. cit.*, p. 105.

23. *Ibid.*, pp. 109–10.

24. *The Proceedings of the Parliament of Scotland Begun at Edinburgh 6th May 1703* [compiled by George Ridpath], Edinburgh, 1704.

25. *The Laws and Acts of Parliament Of Our Most High and Dread Sovereign, Anne, Holden and begun at Edinburgh, the 6 Day of May, 1703,* Edinburgh, 1731, pp. 724–725.

26. Lockhart of Carnwath, *op. cit.*, p. 107.

27. Hume of Crossrigg, *op. cit.*, p. 118.

28. *Letters Relating to Scotland in the Reign of Queen Anne by James Ogilvy, First Earl of Seafield, and Others,* ed. by P. Hume Brown, Edinburgh, 1915, p. 10.

29. Lockhart of Carnwath, *op. cit.*, pp. 56–7.

30. *Ibid.*, pp. 60–2.

31. *Ibid.*, p. 117.

32. Hume of Crossrigg, *ibid.*, pp. 147–8.

33. Lockhart of Carnwath, *op. cit.*, p. 153.

34. Hume of Crossrigg, *op. cit.*, p. 170.

35. Lockhart of Carnwath, *op. cit.*, p. 161.

36. W. C. Mackenzie, *op. cit.*, p. 286; Omond, *op. cit.*, p. 139.

A

DISCOURSE

OF

GOVERNMENT

With relation to

MILITIA'S.

Edinburgh;

Printed in the Year MDCXCVIII.

A DISCOURSE OF GOVERNMENT
WITH RELATION TO
MILITIAS

There is not perhaps in human affairs anything so unaccountable as the indignity and cruelty with which the far greater part of mankind suffer themselves to be used under pretence of government. For some men falsely persuading themselves that bad governments are advantageous to them, as most conducing to gratify their ambition, avarice, and luxury, set themselves with the utmost art and violence to procure their establishment: and by such men almost the whole world has been trampled underfoot, and subjected to tyranny, for want of understanding by what means and methods they were enslaved. For though mankind take great care and pains to instruct themselves in other arts and sciences, yet very few apply themselves to consider the nature of government, an enquiry so useful and necessary both to magistrate and people. Nay, in most countries the arts of state being altogether directed either to enslave the people, or to keep them under slavery; it is become almost everywhere a crime to reason about matters of government. But if men would bestow a small part of the time and application which they throw away upon curious but useless studies, or endless gaming, in perusing those excellent rules and examples of government which the ancients have left us, they would soon be enabled to discover all such abuses and corruptions as tend to the ruin of public societies. It is therefore very strange that they should think study and knowledge necessary in everything they go about, except in the noblest and most useful of all applications, the art of government.

Now if any man in compassion to the miseries of a people should endeavour to disabuse them in anything relating to government, he will certainly incur the displeasure, and perhaps be pursued by the rage of those, who think they find their account in the oppression of the world; but will hardly succeed in his endeavours to undeceive the multitude. For the generality of all ranks of men are cheated by words and names; and provided the ancient terms and outward forms of any government be retained, let the nature of it be never so much altered,

2

they continue to dream that they shall still enjoy their former liberty, and are not to be awakened till it prove too late. Of this there are many remarkable examples in history; but that particular instance which I have chosen to insist on, as most suitable to my purpose, is the alteration of government which happened in most countries of Europe about the year 1500. And it is worth observation, that though this change was fatal to their liberty, yet it was not introduced by the contrivance of ill-designing men; nor were the mischievous consequences perceived, unless perhaps by a few wise men, who, if they saw it, wanted power to prevent it.

Two hundred years being already passed since this alteration began, Europe has felt the effects of it by sad experience; and the true causes of the change are now become more visible.

To lay open this matter in its full extent, it will be necessary to look farther back, and examine the original and constitution of those governments that were established in Europe about the year 400, and continued till this alteration.

When the Goths, Vandals, and other warlike nations had, at different times, and under different leaders, overrun the western parts of the Roman empire, they introduced the following form of government into all the nations they subdued. The general of the army became king of the conquered country; and the conquest being absolute, he divided the lands amongst the great officers of his army, afterwards called barons; who again parcelled out their several territories in smaller portions to the inferior soldiers that had followed them in the wars, and who then became their vassals, enjoying those lands for military service. The king reserved to himself some demesnes for the maintenance of his court and attendance. When this was done, there was no longer any standing army kept on foot, but every man went to live upon his own lands; and when the defence of the country required an army, the king summoned the barons to his standard, who came attended with their vassals. Thus were the armies of Europe composed for about eleven hundred years; and this constitution of government put the sword into the hands of the subject, because the vassals depended more immediately on the barons than on the king, which effectually secured the freedom of those governments. For the barons could not make use of their power to destroy those limited monarchies, without destroying their own grandeur; nor could the king invade their privileges, having no other forces than the vassals of his own demesnes to rely upon for his support in such an attempt.

3

I lay no great stress on any other limitations of those monarchies; nor do I think any so essential to the liberties of the people, as that which placed the sword in the hands of the subject. And since in our time most princes of Europe are in possession of the sword, by standing mercenary forces kept up in time of peace, absolutely depending upon them, I say that all such governments are changed from monarchies to tyrannies. Nor can the power of granting or refusing money, though vested in the subject, be a sufficient security for liberty, where a standing mercenary army is kept up in time of peace: for he that is armed is always master of the purse of him that is unarmed. And not only that government is tyrannical, which is tyrannically exercised; but all governments are tyrannical, which have not in their constitution a sufficient security against the arbitrary power of the prince.

I do not deny that these limited monarchies, during the greatness of the barons, had some defects: I know few governments free from them. But after all, there was a balance that kept those governments steady, and an effectual provision against the encroachments of the crown. I do less pretend that the present governments can be restored to the constitution before-mentioned. The following discourse will show the impossibility of it. My design in the first place is to explain the nature of the past and present governments of Europe, and to disabuse those who think them the same, because they are called by the same names; and who ignorantly clamour against such as would preserve that liberty which is yet left.

In order to this, and for a further and clearer illustration of the matter, I shall deduce from their original, the causes, occasions, and the complication of those many unforeseen accidents; which falling out much about the same time, produced so great a change. And it will at first sight seem very strange, when I shall name the restoration of learning, the invention of printing, of the needle and of gunpowder, as the chief of them; things in themselves so excellent, and which, the last only excepted, might have proved of infinite advantage to the world, if their remote influence upon government had been obviated by suitable remedies. Such odd consequences, and of such a different nature, accompany extraordinary inventions of any kind.

Constantinople being taken by Mahomet the second, in the year 1453, many learned Greeks fled over into Italy; where the favourable reception they found from the popes, princes, and republics of that country, soon introduced amongst the better sort of men, the study of the Greek tongue, and of the ancient authors in that language. About the same time likewise some learned men began to restore the purity of the Latin tongue. But that which most contributed to the advancement of all kind of learning, and especially the study of the ancients, was the art of printing; which was brought to a great degree of perfection a few years after. By this means their books became common, and their arts generally understood and admired. But as mankind from a natural propension to pleasure, is always ready to choose out of everything what may most gratify that vicious appetite; so the arts which the Italians first applied themselves to improve were principally those that had been subservient to the luxury of the ancients in the most corrupt ages, of which they had many monuments still remaining. Italy was presently filled with architects, painters, and sculptors; and a prodigious expense was made in buildings, pictures, and statues. Thus the Italians began to come off from their frugal and military way of living, and addicted themselves to the pursuit of refined and expensive pleasures, as much as the wars of those times would permit. This infection spread itself by degrees into the neighbouring nations. But these things alone had not been sufficient to work so great a change in government, if a preceding invention, brought into common use about that time, had not produced more new and extraordinary effects than any had ever done before; which probably may have many consequences yet unforeseen, and a farther influence upon the manners of men, as long as the world lasts; I mean, the invention of the needle, by the help of which navigation was greatly improved, a passage opened by sea to the East Indies, and a new world discovered. By this means the luxury of Asia and America was added to that of the ancients; and all ages, and all countries concurred, to sink Europe into an abyss of pleasures; which were rendered the more expensive by a perpetual change of the fashions in clothes, equipage, and furniture of houses.

These things brought a total alteration in the way of living, upon which all government depends. It is true, knowledge being mightily increased, and a great curiosity and nicety in everything introduced, men imagined themselves to be gainers in all points, by changing from their frugal and military way of living, which I must confess had some mixture of rudeness and ignorance in it, though not inseparable from it. But at the same time they did not consider the unspeakable evils that are altogether inseparable from an expensive way of living.

To touch upon all these, though slightly, would carry me too far from my subject: I shall therefore content myself to apply what has been said, to the immediate design of this discourse.

5

The far greater share of all those expenses fell upon the barons; for they were the persons most able to make them, and their dignity seemed to challenge whatever might distinguish them from other men. This plunged them on a sudden into so great debts, that if they did not sell, or otherwise alienate their lands, they found themselves at least obliged to turn the military service their vassals owed them into money; partly by way of rent, and partly by way of lease, or fine, for payment of their creditors. And by this means the vassal having his lands no longer at so easy a rate as before, could no more be obliged to military service, and so became a tenant. Thus the armies, which in preceding times had been always composed of such men as these, ceased of course, and the sword fell out of the hands of the barons. But there being always a necessity to provide for the defence of every country, princes were afterwards allowed to raise armies of volunteers and mercenaries. And great sums were given by diets and parliaments for their maintenance, to be levied upon the people grown rich by trade, and dispirited for want of military exercise. Such forces were at first only raised for present exigencies, and continued no longer on foot than the occasions lasted. But princes soon found pretences to make them perpetual, the chief of which was the garrisoning frontier towns and fortresses; the methods of war being altered to the tedious and chargeable way of sieges, principally by the invention of gunpowder. The officers and soldiers of these mercenary armies depending for their subsistence and preferment, as immediately upon the prince, as the former militias did upon the barons, the power of the sword was transferred from the subject to the king, and war grew a constant trade to live by. Nay, many of the barons themselves being reduced to poverty by their expensive way of living, took commands in those mercenary troops; and being still continued hereditary members of diets, and other assemblies of state, after the loss of their vassals, whom they formerly represented, they were now the readiest of all others to load the people with heavy taxes, which were employed to increase the prince's military power, by guards, armies, and citadels, beyond bounds or remedy.

Some princes with much impatience pressed on to arbitrary power before things were ripe, as the kings of France and Charles duke of Burgundy. Philip de Commines says of the latter, 'That having made a truce with the King of France he called an assembly of the estates of his country, and remonstrated to them the prejudice he had sustained by not having standing troops as that king had; that if five hundred men had been in garrison upon their frontier, the king of France would never have undertaken that war; and having represented the mischiefs that were ready to fall upon them for want of such a force, he earnestly pressed them to grant such a sum as would maintain eight hundred lances. At length they gave him a hundred and twenty thousand crowns more than his ordinary revenue (from which tax Burgundy was exempted). But his subjects were for many reasons under great apprehensions of falling into the subjection to which they saw the kingdom of France already reduced by means of such troops. And truly their apprehensions were not ill-grounded; for when he had got together five or six hundred men at arms, he presently had a mind to more, and with them disturbed the peace of all his neighbours: he augmented the tax from one hundred and twenty to five hundred thousand crowns, and increased the numbers of those men at arms, by whom his subjects were greatly oppressed.' Francis de Beaucaire, bishop of Metz, in his history of France speaking of the same affair, says, 'That the foresaid states could not be induced to maintain mercenary forces, being sensible of the difficulties into which the commonalty of France had brought themselves by the like concession; that princes might increase their forces at pleasure, and sometimes (even when they had obtained money) pay them ill, to the vexation and destruction of the poor people; and likewise that kings and princes not contented with their ancient patrimony, were always ready under this pretext to break in upon the properties of all men, and to raise what money they pleased. That nevertheless they gave him a hundred and twenty thousand crowns yearly, which he soon increased to five hundred thousand: but that Burgundy (which was the ancient dominion of that family) retained its ancient liberty, and could by no means be obliged to pay any part of this new tax.' It is true, Philip de Commines subjoins to the forecited passage, that he believes standing forces may be well employed under a wise king or prince; but that if he be not so, or leaves his children young, the use that he or their governors make of them, is not always profitable either for the king or his subjects. If this addition be his own, and not rather an insertion added by the president of the parliament of Paris, who published and, as the foresaid Francis de Beaucaire says he was credibly informed, corrupted his memoirs, yet experience shows him to be mistaken: for the example of his master Louis the eleventh, whom upon many occasions he calls a wise prince, and those of most princes under whom standing forces were first allowed, demonstrates, that they are more dangerous under a wise prince than any other: and reason tells us, that if they are the only proper instruments to introduce arbitrary power, as shall be made plain, a cunning and able prince, who by the world is called a wise one, is more capable of using them to that end than a weak prince, or governors during a minority; and that a wise prince having once procured them to be established, they will maintain themselves under any.

I am not ignorant that before this change, subsidies were often given by diets, states, and parliaments, and some raised by the edicts of princes for maintaining wars; but these were small, and no way sufficient to subsist such numerous armies as those of the barons' militia. There were likewise mercenary troops sometimes entertained by princes who aimed at arbitrary power, and by some commonwealths in time of war for their own defence; but these were only strangers, or in very small numbers, and held no proportion with those vast armies of mercenaries which this change has fixed upon Europe to her affliction and ruin.

What I have said hitherto has been always with regard to one or other, and often to most countries in Europe. What follows will have a more particular regard to Britain; where, though the power of the barons be ceased, yet no mercenary troops are yet established. The reason of which is, that England had before this great alteration lost all her conquests in France, the town of Calais only excepted; and that also was taken by the French before the change was thoroughly made. So that the Kings of England had no pretence to keep up standing forces, either to defend conquests abroad or to garrison a frontier towards France, since the sea was now become the only frontier between those two countries.

Neither could the frontier towards Scotland afford any colour to those princes for raising such forces, since the Kings of Scotland had none; and that Scotland was not able to give money for the subsisting any considerable number. It is true, the example of France, with which country Scotland had constant correspondence, and some French counsellors about Mary of Guise, Queen dowager and regent of Scotland, induced her to propose a tax for the subsisting of mercenary soldiers to be employed for the defence of the frontier of Scotland; and to ease, as was pretended, the barons of that trouble. But in that honourable and wise remonstrance, which was made by three hundred of the lesser barons (as much dissatisfied with the lords, who by their silence betrayed the public liberty, as with the Regent herself) she was

8

told, that their forefathers had defended themselves and their fortunes against the English, when that nation was much more powerful than they were at that time, and had made frequent incursions into their country: that they themselves had not so far degenerated from their ancestors, to refuse, when occasion required, to hazard their lives and fortunes in the service of their country: that as to the hiring of mercenary soldiers, it was a thing of great danger to put the liberty of Scotland into the hands of men, who are of no fortunes, nor have any hopes but in the public calamity; who for money would attempt anything; whose excessive avarice opportunity would inflame to a desire of all manner of innovations, and whose faith would follow the wheel of fortune. That though these men should be more mindful of the duty they owe to their country, than of their own particular interest, was it to be supposed, that mercenaries would fight more bravely for the defence of other men's fortunes, than the possessors would do for themselves or their own; or that a little money should excite their ignoble minds to a higher pitch of honour than that with which the barons are inspired, when they fight for the preservation of their fortunes, wives and children, religion and liberty: that most men did suspect and apprehend, that this new way of making war, might be not only useless, but dangerous to the nation; since the English, if they should imitate the example, might, without any great trouble to their people, raise far greater sums for the maintenance of mercenary soldiers, than Scotland could, and by this means not only spoil and lay open the frontier, but penetrate into the bowels of the kingdom: and that it was in the militia of the barons their ancestors had placed their chief trust, for the defence of themselves against a greater power.

By these powerful reasons being made sensible of her error, the Queen desisted from her demands. Her daughter Queen Mary, who, as the great historian says, looked upon the moderate government of a limited kingdom, to be disgraceful to monarchs, and upon the slavery of the people, as the freedom of kings, resolved to have guards about her person; but could not fall upon a way to compass them: for she could find no pretext, unless it were the empty show of magnificence which belongs to a court, and the example of foreign princes; for the former kings had always trusted themselves to the faith of the barons. At length upon a false and ridiculous pretence, of an intention in a certain nobleman to seize her person, she assumed them; but they were soon abolished. Nor had her son King James any other guards whilst he was King of Scotland only, than forty gentlemen: and that

9

King declares in the act of parliament, by which they are established, that he will not burden his people by any tax or imposition for their maintenance.

Henry the seventh, King of England, seems to have perceived sooner, and understood better the alteration before-mentioned, than any prince of his time, and obtained several laws to favour and facilitate it. But his successors were altogether improper to second him: for Henry the eighth was an unthinking prince. The reigns of Edward the sixth and Queen Mary were short; and Queen Elizabeth loved her people too well to attempt it. King James, who succeeded her, was a stranger in England, and of no interest abroad. King Charles the first did indeed endeavour to make himself absolute, though somewhat preposterously; for he attempted to seize the purse, before he was master of the sword. But very wise men have been of opinion, that if he had been possessed of as numerous guards as those which were afterwards raised, and constantly kept up by King Charles the second, he might easily have succeeded in his enterprise. For we see that in those struggles which the country party had with King Charles the second, and in those endeavours they used to bring about that revolution which was afterwards compassed by a foreign power, the chief and insuperable difficulty they met with, was from those guards. And though King James the second had provoked these nations to the last degree, and made his own game as hard as possible, not only by invading our civil liberties, but likewise by endeavouring to change the established religion for another which the people abhorred, whereby he lost their affections, and even those of a great part of his army: yet notwithstanding all this mismanagement, Britain stood in need of a foreign force to save it; and how dangerous a remedy that is, the histories of all ages can witness. It is true, this circumstance was favourable, that a prince who had married the next heir to these kingdoms, was at the head of our deliverance: yet did it engage us in a long and expensive war. And now that we are much impoverished, and England by means of her former riches and present poverty, fallen into all the corruptions which those great enemies of virtue, want, and excess of riches can produce; that there are such numbers of mercenary forces on foot at home and abroad; that the greatest part of the officers have no other way to subsist; that they are commanded by a wise and active King, who has at his disposal the formidable land and sea forces of a neighbouring nation, the great rival of our trade; a King, who by blood, relation, other particular ties, and common interest, has the house of

Austria, most of the princes of Germany, and potentates of the North, for his friends and allies; who can, whatever interest he join with, do what he thinks fit in Europe; I say, if a mercenary standing army be kept up (the first of that kind, except those of the usurper Cromwell, and the late King James, that Britain has seen for thirteen hundred years) I desire to know where the security of the British liberties lies, unless in the good will and pleasure of the King: I desire to know, what real security can be had against standing armies of mercenaries, backed by the corruption of both nations, the tendency of the way of living, the genius of the age, and the example of the world.

Having shown the difference between the past and present government of Britain, how precarious our liberties are, and how from having the best security for them we are in hazard of having none at all; it is to be hoped that those who are for a standing army, and losing no occasion of advancing and extending the prerogative, from a mistaken opinion that they establish the ancient government of these nations, will see what sort of patriots they are.

But we are told, that only standing mercenary forces can defend Britain from the perpetual standing armies of France. However frivolous this assertion be, as indeed no good argument can be brought to support it, either from reason or experience, as shall be proved hereafter; yet allowing it to be good, what security can the nations have that these standing forces shall not at some time or other be made use of to suppress the liberties of the people, though not in this king's time, to whom we owe their preservation? For I hope there is no man so weak to think, that keeping up the army for a year, or for any longer time than the parliaments of both nations shall have engaged the public faith to make good all deficiencies of funds granted for their maintenance, is not the keeping them up for ever. It is a pitiful shift in the undertakers for a standing army, to say, we are not for a standing army, we are only for an army from year to year, or till the militia be made useful. For Britain cannot be in any hazard from France; at least till that kingdom, so much exhausted by war and persecution, shall have a breathing space to recover. Before that time our militias will be in order; and in the meantime the fleet. Besides, no prince ever surrendered so great countries and so many strong places, I shall not say, in order to make a new war; but as these men will have it, to continue the same. The French King is old and diseased, and was never willing to hazard much by any bold attempt. If he, or the dauphin, upon his decease, may be suspected of any farther design, it must be upon the Spanish monarchy, in case of the death of that King. And if it be objected, that we shall stand in need of an army, in such a conjuncture, I answer, that our part in that, or in any other foreign war, will be best managed by sea, as shall be shown hereafter.

Let us then see if mercenary armies be not exactly calculated to enslave a nation. Which I think may be easily proved, if we consider that such troops are generally composed of men who make a trade of war; and having little or no patrimony, or spent what they once had, enter into that employment in hopes of its continuance during life, not at all thinking how to make themselves capable of any other. By which means heavy and perpetual taxes must be entailed for ever upon the people for their subsistence; and since all their relations stand engaged to support their interest, let all men judge, if this will not prove a very united and formidable party in a nation.

But the undertakers must pardon me if I tell them, that no well-constituted government ever suffered any such men in it, whose interest leads them to embroil the state in war, and are a useless and insupportable burden in time of peace. Venice or Holland are neither of them examples to prove the contrary; for had not their situation been different from that of other countries, their liberty had not continued to this time. And they suffer no forces to remain within those inaccessible places, which are the chief seats of their power. Carthage, that had not those advantages of situation, and yet used mercenary forces, was brought to the brink of ruin by them in a time of peace, beaten in three wars, and at last subdued by the Romans. If ever any government stood in need of such a sort of men, it was that of ancient Rome, because they were engaged in perpetual war. The argument can never be so strong in any other case. But the Romans well knowing such men and liberty to be incompatible, and yet being under a necessity of having armies constantly on foot, made frequent changes of the men that served in them; who, when they had been some time in the army, were permitted to return to their possessions, trades, or other employments. And to show how true a judgment that wise state made of this matter, it is sufficient to observe, that those who subverted that government, the greatest that ever was amongst men, found themselves obliged to continue the same soldiers always in constant pay and service.

If during the late war we had followed so wise a course as that of Rome, there had been thrice as many trained men in the nations as at present there are; no difficulties about recruits, nor debates about keeping up armies in time of peace, because some men resolve to live by arms in time of peace, whether it be for the good of the nations or not. And since such was the practice of Rome, I hope no man will have the confidence to say that this method was not as effectual for war as any other. If it be objected that Rome had perpetual wars, and therefore that might be a good practice among them, which would not be so with us, I confess I cannot see the consequence; for if Rome had perpetual wars, the Romans ought still to have continued the same men in their armies, that they might, according to the notion of these men, render their troops more useful. And if we did change our men during a war, we should have more men that would understand something of it. If any man say, not so much as if they continued in the army: I answer, that many of those who continue in the army are afterwards swept away by the war, and live not to be of use in time of peace; that those who escape the war, being fewer than in the other case, are soon consumed: and that mercenary standing forces in time of peace, if not employed to do mischief, soon become like those of Holland in 72, fit only to lose forty strong places in forty days.

There is another thing which I would not mention if it were not absolutely necessary to my present purpose; and that is, the usual manners of those who are engaged in mercenary armies. I speak now of officers in other parts of Europe, and not of those in our armies, allowing them to be the best, and if they will have it so, quite different from all others. I will not apply to them any part of what I shall say concerning the rest. They themselves best know how far anything of that nature may be applicable to them. I say then, most princes of Europe having put themselves upon the foot of keeping up forces, rather numerous than well entertained, can give but small allowance to officers, and that likewise is for the most part very ill paid, in order to render them the more necessitous and depending; and yet they permit them to live in all that extravagancy which mutual example and emulation prompts them to. By which means the officers become insensibly engaged in numberless frauds, oppressions, and cruelties, the colonels against the captains, and the captains against the inferior soldiers; and all of them against all persons with whom they have any kind of business. So that there is hardly any sort of men who are less men of honour than the officers of mercenary forces: and indeed honour has now no other signification amongst them than courage. Besides, most men that enter into those armies, whether officers or soldiers, as if they were obliged to show themselves new creatures, and perfectly regenerate, if before they were modest or sober, immediately turn themselves to all manner of debauchery and wickedness, committing all kinds of injustice and barbarity against poor and defenceless people. Now though the natural temper of our men be more just and honest than that of the French, or of any other people, yet may it not be feared, that such bad manners may prove contagious? And if such manners do not fit men to enslave a nation, devils only must do it. On the other hand, if it should happen that the officers of standing armies in Britain should live with greater regularity and modesty than was ever yet seen in that sort of men, it might very probably fall out, that being quartered in all parts of the country, some of them might be returned members of parliament for divers of the electing boroughs; and of what consequence that would be, I leave all men to judge. So that whatever be the conduct of a mercenary army, we can never be secure as long as any such force is kept up in Britain.

But the undertakers for a standing army will say: will you turn so many gentlemen to starve, who have faithfully served the government? This question I allow to be founded upon some reason. For it ought to be acknowledged in justice to our soldiery, that on all occasions, and in all actions, both officers and soldiers have done their part; and therefore I think it may be reasonable, that all officers and soldiers of above forty years, in consideration of their unfitness to apply themselves at that age to any other employment, should be recommended to the bounty of both parliaments.

I confess I do not see by what rules of good policy any mercenary forces have been connived at either in Scotland, England, or Ireland. Sure, it is allowing the dispensing power in the most essential point of the constitution of government in these nations.

Scotland and England are nations that were formerly very jealous of liberty; of which there are many remarakble instances in the histories of these countries. And we may hope that the late revolution having given such a blow to arbitrary power in these kingdoms, they will be very careful to preserve their rights and privileges. And sure it is not very suitable to these, that any standing forces be kept up in Britain: or that there should be any Scots, English, or Irish regiments maintained in Ireland, or anywhere abroad; or regiments of any nation at the charge of England. I shall not say how readily the regiments that were in the service of Holland came over against the duke of Monmouth: he was a rebel, and did not succeed. But we all know with what expedition the Irish mercenary forces were brought into Britain to oppose his present majesty in that glorious enterprise for our deliverance.

The subjects formerly had a real security for their liberty, by having the sword in their own hands. That security, which is the greatest of all others, is lost; and not only so, but the sword is put into the hand of the king by his power over the militia. All this is not enough; but we must have in both kingdoms standing armies of mercenaries, who for the most part have no other way to subsist, and consequently are capable to execute any commands: and yet every man must think his liberties as safe as ever, under pain of being thought disaffected to the monarchy. But sure it must not be the ancient limited and legal monarchies of Scotland and England that these gentlemen mean. It must be a French fashion of monarchy, where the king has power to do what he pleases, and the people no security for anything they possess. We have quitted our ancient security, and put the militia into the power of the king. The only remaining security we have is, that no standing armies were ever yet allowed in time of peace, the parliament of England having so often and so expressly declared them to be contrary to law: and that of Scotland having not only declared them to be a grievance, but made the keeping them up an article in the forfeiture of the late King James. If a standing army be allowed, what difference will there be between the government we shall then live under, and any kind of government under a good prince? Of which there have been some in the most despotic tyrannies. If these be limited and not absolute monarchies, then, as there are conditions, so there ought to be securities on both sides. The barons never pretended that their militias should be constantly on foot, and together in bodies in times of peace. It is evident that would have subverted the constitution, and made every one of them a petty tyrant. And it is as evident, that standing forces are the fittest instruments to make a tyrant. Whoever is for making the king's power too great or too little, is an enemy to the monarchy. But to give him standing armies, puts his power beyond control, and consequently makes him absolute. If the people had any other real security for their liberty than that there be no standing armies in time of peace, there might be some colour to demand them. But if that only remaining security be taken away from the people, we have destroyed these monarchies.

It is pretended we are in hazard of being invaded by a powerful enemy; shall we therefore destroy our government? What is it then that we would defend? Is it our persons, by the ruin of our government? In what then shall we be gainers? In saving our lives by the loss of our liberties? If our pleasures and luxury make us live like brutes, it seems we must not pretend to reason any better than they. I would fain know, if there be any other way of making a prince absolute, than by allowing him a standing army: if by it all princes have not been made absolute; if without it, any. Whether our enemies shall conquer us is uncertain; but whether standing armies will enslave us, neither reason nor experience will suffer us to doubt. It is therefore evident that no pretence of danger from abroad can be an argument to keep up standing armies or any mercenary forces.

Let us now consider whether we may not be able to defend ourselves by well-regulated militias against any foreign force, though never so formidable: that these nations may be free from the fears of invasion from abroad, as well as from the danger of slavery at home.

After the barons had lost the military service of their vassals, militias of some kind or other were established in most parts of Europe. But the prince having everywhere the power of naming and preferring the officers of these militias, they could be no balance in government as the former were. And he that will consider what has been said in this discourse, will easily perceive that the essential quality requisite to such a militia, as might fully answer the ends of the former, must be, that the officers should be named and preferred, as well as they and the soldiers paid, by the people that set them out. So that if princes look upon the present militias as not capable of defending a nation against foreign armies, the people have little reason to entrust them with the defence of their liberties.

And though upon the dissolution of that ancient militia under the barons, which made these nations so great and glorious, by setting up militias generally through Europe, the sword came not into the hands of the Commons, which was the only thing could have continued the former balance of government, but was everywhere put into the hands of the king: nevertheless ambitious princes, who aimed at absolute power, thinking they could never use it effectually to that end, unless it were wielded by mercenaries, and men that had no other interest in the commonwealth than their pay, have still endeavoured by all means to discredit militias, and render them burdensome to the people, by never suffering them to be upon any right, or so much as tolerable foot, and all to persuade the necessity of standing forces. And indeed they have succeeded too well in this design: for the greatest part of the world has been fooled into an opinion that a militia cannot be made serviceable. I shall not say it was only militias could conquer the world; and that princes to have succeeded fully in the design before-mentioned must have destroyed all the history and memory of ancient governments, where the accounts of so many excellent models of militia are yet extant. I know the prejudice and ignorance of the world concerning the art of war, as it was practised by the ancients; though what remains of that knowledge in their writings be sufficient to give a mean opinion of the modern discipline. For this reason I shall examine, by what has passed of late years in these nations, whether experience have convinced us, that officers bred in foreign wars, be so far preferable to others who have been under no other discipline than that of an ordinary and ill-regulated militia; and if the commonalty of both kingdoms, at their first entrance upon service, be not as capable of a resolute military action, as any standing forces. This doubt will be fully resolved, by considering the actions of the marquis of Montrose, which may be compared, all circumstances considered, with those of Caesar, as well for the military skill, as the bad tendency of them; though the marquis had never served abroad, nor seen any action, before the six victories, which, with numbers much inferior to those of his enemies, he obtained in one year; and the most considerable of them were chiefly gained by the assistance of the tenants and vassals of the family of Gordon. The battle of Naseby will be a farther illustration of this matter, which is generally thought to have been the deciding action of the late civil war. The number of forces was equal on both sides; nor was there any advantage in the ground, or extraordinary accident that happened during the fight, which could be of considerable importance to either. In the army of the parliament, nine only of the officers had served abroad, and most of the soldiers were prentices drawn out of London but two months before. In the king's army there were above a thousand officers that had served in foreign parts: yet was that army routed and broken by those new-raised prentices; who were observed to be obedient to command, and brave in fight; not only in that action, but on all occasions during that active campaign. The people of these nations are not a dastardly crew, like those born in misery under oppression and slavery, who must have time to rub off that fear, cowardice, and stupidity which they bring from home. And though officers seem to stand in more need of experience than private soldiers; yet in that battle it was seen that the sobriety and principle of the officers on the one side, prevailed over the experience of those on the other.

It is well known that divers regiments of our army, lately in Flanders, have never been once in action, and not one half of them above thrice, nor any of them five times during the whole war. Oh, but they have been under discipline, and accustomed to obey! And so may men in militias. We have had to do with an enemy, who, though abounding in numbers of excellent officers, yet durst never fight us without a visible advantage. Is that enemy like to invade us, when he must be unavoidably necessitated to put all to hazard in ten days, or starve?

A good militia is of such importance to a nation, that it is the chief part of the constitution of any free government. For though as to other things, the constitution be never so slight, a good militia will always preserve the public liberty. But in the best constitution that ever was, as to all other parts of government, if the militia be not upon a right foot, the liberty of that people must perish. The militia of ancient Rome, the best that ever was in any government, made her mistress of the world: but standing armies enslaved that great people, and their excellent militia and freedom perished together. The Lacedemonians continued eight hundred years free, and in great honour, because they had a good militia. The Swisses at this day are the freest, happiest, and the people of all Europe who can best defend themselves, because they have the best militia.

I have shown that liberty in the monarchical governments of Europe, subsisted so long as the militia of the barons was on foot: and that on the decay of their militia (which though it was none of the best, so was it none of the worst) standing forces and tyranny have been everywhere introduced, unless in Britain and Ireland; which by reason of their situation, having the sea for frontier, and a powerful fleet to protect them, could afford no pretence for such forces. And though any militia, however slightly constituted, be sufficient for that reason to defend us; yet all improvements in the constitution of militias, being further securities for the liberty of the people, I think we ought to endeavour the amendment of them, and till that can take place, to make the present militias useful in the former and ordinary methods.

That the whole free people of any nation ought to be exercised to arms, not only the example of our ancestors, as appears by the acts of parliament made in both kingdoms to that purpose, and that of the wisest governments among the ancients; but the advantage of choosing out of great numbers, seems clearly to demonstrate. For in countries where husbandry, trade, manufactures, and other mechanical arts are carried on, even in time of war, the impediments of men are so many and so various, that unless the whole people be exercised, no considerable numbers of men can be drawn out, without disturbing those employments, which are the vitals of the political body. Besides, that upon great defeats, and under extreme calamities, from which no government was ever exempted, every nation stands in need of all the people, as the ancients sometimes did of their slaves. And I cannot see why arms should be denied to any man who is not a slave, since they are the only true badges of liberty; and ought never, but in times of utmost necessity, to be put into the hands of mercenaries or slaves: neither can I understand why any man that has arms should not be taught the use of them.

By the constitution of the present militia in both nations, there is but a small number of the men able to bear arms exercised; and men of quality and estate are allowed to send any wretched servant in their place: so that they themselves are become mean, by being disused to handle arms; and will not learn the use of them, because they are ashamed of their ignorance: by which means the militias being composed only of servants, these nations seem altogether unfit to defend themselves, and standing forces to be necessary. Now can it be supposed that a few servants will fight for the defence of their masters' estates, if their masters only look on? Or that some inconsiderate freeholders, as for the most part those who command the militia are, should, at the head of those servants, expose their lives for men of more plentiful estates, without being assisted by them? No bodies of military men can be of any force or value, unless many persons of quality or education be among them; and such men should blush to think of excusing themselves from serving their country, at least for some years, in a military capacity, if they consider that every Roman was obliged to spend fifteen years of his life in their armies. Is it not a shame that any man who possesses an estate, and is at the same time healthful and young, should not fit himself by all means for the defence of that, and his country, rather than to pay taxes to maintain a mercenary, who though he may defend him during a war, will be sure to insult and enslave him in time of peace. Men must not think that any country can be in a constant posture of defence, without some trouble and charge; but certainly it is better to undergo this, and to preserve

19

our liberty with honour, than to be subjected to heavy taxes, and yet have it insolently ravished from us, to our present oppression, and the lasting misery of our posterity. But it will be said, where are the men to be found who shall exercise all this people in so many several places at once? for the nobility and gentry know nothing of the matter; and to hire so many soldiers of fortune, as they call them, will be chargeable, and may be dangerous, these men being all mercenaries, and always the same men, in the same trusts: besides that the employing such men would not be suitable to the design of breeding the men of quality and estate to command, as well as the others to obey.

To obviate these difficulties, and because the want of a good model of militia, and a right method for training people in time of peace, so as they need not apprehend any war, though never so sudden, is at this day the bane of the liberty of Europe, I shall propose one, accommodated to the invincible difficulty of bringing men of quality and estate, or men of any rank, who have passed the time of youth, to the use of arms; and new, because though we have many excellent models of militia, delivered to us by ancient authors, with respect to the use of them in time of war, yet they give us but little information concerning the methods by which they trained their whole people for war in time of peace; so that if the model which I shall propose have not the authority of the ancients to recommend it, yet perhaps by a severe discipline, and a right method of disposing the minds of men, as well as forming their bodies, for military and virtuous actions, it may have some resemblance of their excellent institutions.

What I would offer is, that four camps be formed, one in Scotland, and three in England; into which all the young men of the respective countries should enter, on the first day of the two and twentieth year of their age; and remain there the space of two years, if they be of fortunes sufficient to maintain themselves; but if they are not, then to remain a year only, at the expense of the public. In this camp they should be taught the use of all sorts of arms, with the necessary evolutions; as also wrestling, leaping, swimming, and the like exercises. He whose condition would permit him to buy and maintain a horse, should be obliged so to do, and be taught to vault, to ride, and to manage his own horse. This camp should seldom remain above eight days in one place, but remove from heath to heath; not only upon the account of cleanliness and health, but to teach the youth to fortify a camp, to march, and to accustom them (respect being always had to those of a weak constitution) to carry as much in their march as ever

20

any Roman soldier did; that is to say, their tents, provision, arms, armour, their utensils, and the palisades of their camp. They should be taught to forage, and be obliged to use the countrymen with all justice in their bargains, for that and all other things they stand in need of from them. The food of every man within the camp should be the same; for bread they should have only wheat, which they are to be obliged to grind with hand-mills; they should have some salt, and a certain number of beeves allowed them at certain times of the year. Their drink should be water, sometimes tempered with a proportion of brandy, and at other times with vinegar. Their clothes should be plain, coarse, and of a fashion fitted in everything for the fatigue of a camp. For all these things those who could should pay; and those who could not should be defrayed by the public, as has been said. The camp should be sometimes divided into two parts, which should remove from each other many miles, and should break up again at the same time, in order to meet upon some mountainous, marshy, woody, or in a word, cross ground; that not only their diligence, patience, and suffering in marches, but their skill in seizing of grounds, posting bodies of horse and foot, and advancing towards each other; their choosing a camp, and drawing out of it in order to a battle, might be seen, as well as what orders of battle they would form upon the variety of different grounds. The persons of quality or estate should likewise be instructed in fortification, gunnery, and all things belonging to the duty of an engineer: and forts should be sometimes built by the whole camp, where all the arts of attacking and defending places should be practised. The youth having been taught to read at schools, should be obliged to read at spare hours some excellent histories, but chiefly those in which military actions are best described; with the books that have been best written concerning the military art. Speeches exhorting to military and virtuous actions should be often composed, and pronounced publicly by such of the youth as were, by education and natural talents, qualified for it. There being none but military men allowed within the camp, and no churchmen being of that number, such of the youth as may be fit to exhort the rest to all Christian and moral duties, chiefly to humility, modesty, charity, and the pardoning of private injuries, should be chosen to do it every Sunday, and the rest of that day spent in reading books, and in conversation directed to the same end. And all this under so severe and rigorous orders, attended with so exact an execution by reward and punishment, that no officer within the camp should have the power of pardoning the one, or withholding the other.

The rewards should be all honorary, and contrived to suit the nature of the different good qualities and degrees in which any of the youth had shown, either his modesty, obedience, patience in suffering, temperance, diligence, address, invention, judgment, temper, or valour. The punishments should be much more rigorous than those inflicted for the same crimes by the law of the land. And there should be punishments for some things, not liable to any by the common law, immodest and insolent words or actions, gaming, and the like. No woman should be suffered to come within the camp, and the crimes of abusing their own bodies any manner of way, punished with death. All these things to be judged by their own councils of war; and those councils to have for rule, certain articles drawn up and approved by the respective parliaments. The officers and masters, for instructing and teaching the youth, in all the exercises above-mentioned, should upon the first establishment of such a camp, be the most expert men in those disciplines; and brought by encouragements from all places of Europe; due care being taken that they should not infect the youth with foreign manners. But afterwards they ought to consist of such men of quality or fortune as should be chosen for that end, out of those who had formerly passed two years in the camp, and since that time had improved themselves in the wars; who upon their return should be obliged to serve two years in that station. As for the numbers of those officers, or masters; their several duties; that of the camp-master-general, and of the commissaries; the times and manner of exercise, with divers other particulars of less consideration, and yet necessary to be determined, in order to put such a design in execution, for brevity's sake I omit them, as easy to be resolved. But certainly it were no hard matter, for men that had passed through such a discipline as that of the camp I have described, to retain it after they should return to their several homes; if the people of every town and village, together with those of the adjacent habitations, were obliged to meet fifty times in the year, on such days as should be found most convenient; and exercise four hours every time: for all men being instructed in what they are to do; and the men of quality and estate most knowing, and expert of all others, the exercise might be performed in great perfection. There might also be yearly in the summer time, a camp of some thousands of the nearest neighbours brought and kept together for a week to do those exercises, which cannot be performed in any other place: every man of a certain estate being obliged to keep a horse fit for the war. By this means it would be easy upon any occasion, though

22

never so small (as for example, the keeping of the peace, and putting the laws in execution where force is necessary) or never so great and sudden (as upon account of invasions and conspiracies) to bring together such numbers of officers and soldiers as the exigence required, according to the practice of ancient Rome; which in this particular might be imitated by us without difficulty: and if such a method were once established, there would be no necessity of keeping up a militia formed into regiments of foot and horse in time of peace. Now if this militia should stand in need of any farther improvement (because no militias seem comparable to those exercised in actual war; as that of the barons by their constant feuds; and that of Rome, and some other ancient commonwealths, by their perpetual wars) a certain small number of forces might be employed in any foreign country where there should be action; a fourth part of which might be changed every year; that all those who had in this manner acquired experience, might be dispersed among the several regiments of any army, that the defence of these countries should at any time call for; which would serve to confirm and give assurance to the rest. Such a militia would be of no great expense to these nations; for the mean clothing and provisions for those who could not maintain themselves, being given only for one year, would amount to little; and no other expense would be needful, except for their arms, a small train of artillery for each camp, and what is to be given for the encouragement of the first officers and masters.

A militia upon such a foot would have none of the infinite and insuperable difficulties there are, to bring a few men who live at a great distance from one another, frequently together to exercise; at which consequently they must be from home every time several days: of finding such a number of masters, as are necessary to train so many thousands of people ignorant of all exercise, in so many different places, and for the most part at the same time: it would have none of those innumerable incumbrances, and unnecessary expenses, with which a militia formed into regiments of foot and horse in time of peace is attended. In such a camp the youth would not only be taught the exercise of a musket with a few evolutions, which is all that men in ordinary militias pretend to, and is the least part of the duty of a soldier; but besides a great many exercises to strengthen and dispose the body for fight, they would learn to fence, to ride, and manage a horse for the war; to forage and live in a camp; to fortify, attack, and defend any place; and what is no less necessary, to undergo the greatest toils, and to give obedience to the severest orders. Such a militia, by sending beyond seas certain proportions of it, and relieving them from time to time, would enable us to assist our allies more powerfully than by standing armies we could ever do. Such a camp would take away the great difficulty of bringing men of all conditions, who have passed the time of their youth, to apply themselves to the use and exercise of arms; and beginning with them early, when like wax they may be moulded into any shape, would dispose them to place their greatest honour in the performance of those exercises, and inspire them with the fires of military glory, to which that age is so inclined; which impression being made upon their youth, would last as long as life. Such a camp would be as great a school of virtue as of military discipline: in which the youth would learn to stand in need of few things; to be content with that small allowance which nature requires; to suffer, as well as to act; to be modest, as well as brave; to be as much ashamed of doing anything insolent or injurious, as of turning their back upon an enemy; they would learn to forgive injuries done to themselves, but to embrace with joy the occasions of dying to revenge those done to their country: and virtue imbibed in younger years would cast a flavour to the utmost periods of life. In a word, they would learn greater and better things than the military art, and more necessary too, if anything can be more necessary than the defence of our country. Such a militia might not only defend a people living in an island, but even such as are placed in the midst of the most warlike nations of the world.

Now till such a militia may be brought to some perfection, our present militia is not only sufficient to defend us; but considering the circumstances of the French affairs, especially with relation to Spain, Britain cannot justly apprehend an invasion, if the fleet of England, to which Scotland furnished during the late war seven or eight thousand seamen, were in such order as it ought to be. And it can never be the interest of these nations to take any other share in preserving the balance of Europe, than what may be performed by our fleet. By which means our money will be spent amongst ourselves; our trade preserved to support the charge of the navy; our enemies totally driven out of the sea, and great numbers of their forces diverted from opposing the armies of our allies abroad, to the defence of their own coasts.

If this method had been taken in the late war, I presume it would have proved not only more advantageous to us, but also more serviceable to our allies than that which was followed. And it is in vain to say, that at this rate we shall have no allies at all: for the weaker party on the Continent must be contented to accept our assistance in the manner we think fit to give it, or inevitably perish. But if we send any forces beyond the seas to join those of our allies, they ought to be part of our militia, as has been said, and not standing forces; otherwise, at the end of every war, the present struggle will recur, and at one time or other these nations will be betrayed, and a standing army established: so that nothing can save us from following the fate of all the other kingdoms in Europe, but putting our trust altogether in our fleet and militias, and having no other forces than these. The sea is the only empire which can naturally belong to us. Conquest is not our interest, much less to consume our people and treasure in conquering for others.

To conclude; if we seriously consider the happy condition of these nations, who have lived so long under the blessings of liberty, we cannot but be affected with the most tender compassion to think that the Scots, who have for so many ages, with such resolution, defended their liberty against the Picts, Britons, Romans, Saxons, Danes, Irish, Normans, and English, as well as against the violence and tyranny of so many of their own princes; that the English, who, whatever revolutions their country has been subject to, have still maintained their rights and liberties against all attempts; who possess a country, everywhere cultivated and improved by the industry of rich husbandmen; her rivers and harbours filled with ships; her cities, towns, and villages enriched with manufactures; where men of vast estates live in secure possession of them, and whose merchants live in as great splendour as the nobility of other nations: that Scotland which has a gentry born to excel in arts and arms: that England which has a commonalty, not only surpassing all those of that degree which the world can now boast of, but also those of all former ages, in courage, honesty, good sense, industry, and generosity of temper; in whose very looks there are such visible marks of a free and liberal education; which advantages cannot be imputed to the climate, or to any other cause, but the freedom of the government under which they live: I say, it cannot but make the hearts of all honest men bleed to think, that in their days the felicity and liberties of such countries must come to a period, if the parliaments do not prevent it, and his majesty be not prevailed upon to lay aside the thoughts of mercenary armies, which, if once established, will inevitably produce those fatal consequences that have always attended such forces in the other kingdoms of Europe; violation of property, decay of trade, oppression of the country by heavy taxes and quarters, the utmost misery and slavery of the poorer sort, the ruin of the nobility by their expenses in court and army, deceit and treachery in all ranks of men, occasioned by want and necessity. Then shall we see the gentry of Scotland, ignorant through want of education, and cowardly by being oppressed; then shall we see the once happy commonalty of England become base and abject, by being continually exposed to the brutal insolence of the soldiers; the women debauched by their lust; ugly and nasty through poverty, and the want of things necessary to preserve their natural beauty. Then shall we see that great city, the pride and glory, not only of our island, but of the world, subjected to the excessive impositions Paris now lies under, and reduced to a peddling trade, serving only to foment the luxury of a court. Then will Britain know what obligations she has to those who are for mercenary armies.

TWO

DISCOURSES

Concerning the

AFFAIRS

OF

SCOTLAND;

Written in the Year 1698.

Edinburgh, 1698.

THE FIRST
DISCOURSE

No inclination is so honourable, nor has anything been so much esteemed in all nations, and ages, as the love of that country and society in which every man is born. And those who have placed their greatest satisfaction in doing good, have accounted themselves happy, or unfortunate, according to the success of their endeavours to serve the interest of their country. For nothing can be more powerful in the minds of men, than a natural inclination and duty concurring in the same disposition.

Nature in most men prevails over reason; reason in some prevails over nature: but when these two are joined, and a violent natural inclination finds itself owned by reason, required by duty, encouraged by the highest praises, and excited by the most illustrious examples, sure that force must be irresistible. Constrained by so great a force, and the circumstances of my affairs not allowing me to be otherwise serviceable to my country, I have in the following discourse given my opinion concerning divers matters of importance, which probably may be debated in the approaching session of parliament. I shall be very well satisfied if anything I say do afford a hint that may be improved by men of better judgment to the public good. I hope I shall not be blamed for giving my opinion in matters of public concernment, since it is the right and duty of every man to write or speak his mind freely in all things that may come before any parliament; to the end that they who represent the nation in that assembly may be truly informed of the sentiments of those they represent. Besides, we are now no more under those tyrannical reigns in which it was a crime to speak of public affairs, or to say that the king had received bad counsel in anything. If in this discourse I argue against some things, which perhaps may not be proposed in the ensuing session of parliament, they are nevertheless such as persons in public trust have in their conversation given just cause to think they were designed.

It is probable that the parliament, before they proceed to any other business, will take into consideration a transaction, which having passed since the last session, may, if it be not abolished, import no less than the infringing the freedom of this and all subsequent parliaments; I mean, the farming of the customs to the state of burghs.

Corruption is so entirely disowned by all men, that I may be allowed to say, when I name it, that I name the blackest of crimes; and when I name any guilty of it, I name a very odious criminal. But corruption is more or less dangerous in proportion to the stations in which corrupt men are placed. When a private man receives any advantage to betray a trust, one or a few persons may suffer; if a judge be corrupted, the oppression is extended to greater numbers: but when legislators are bribed, or (which is all one) are under any particular engagement, that may influence them in their legislative capacity, much more when an entire state of parliament is brought under those circumstances, then it is that we must expect injustice to be established by a law, and all those consequences which will inevitably follow the subversion of a constitution, I mean, standing armies, oppressive taxes, slavery; whilst the outward form only of the ancient government remains to give them authority. I confess I have been often struck with astonishment, and could never make an end of admiring the folly and stupidity of men living under some modern governments, who will exclaim against a judge that takes bribes, and never rest till he be punished, or at least removed; and yet at the same time suffer great numbers of those who have the legislative authority to receive the constant bribes of places and pensions to betray them. But we shall have less to say for ourselves if we suffer the votes of the whole state of burghs to be at once influenced by the farming of the customs. For in other places the impudence of bribery has gone no farther than to attack single persons; but to endeavour at once to bribe a whole state of parliament, is an attempt of which it seems we only are capable.

Yet to show how far I am from suspecting any man of the least bad design, without a cause, I shall say, that as I know this business of the farm above-mentioned was first moved without any design to influence the votes of the burghs in parliament; so I am willing to believe that few of those who have since acted in this affair had any such design. But if any man, after due consideration of the evil consequences which must follow, and are inseparable from such a farm, shall still persist in endeavouring to continue it, he cannot but be an enemy to the liberties of his country.

This is so bold an attempt, and so inconsistent with the freedom of parliament, that till it be removed it is to be presumed they will not proceed to any other business: but this obstruction once taken away, we may hope they will begin with that affair which presses most, and in which the nation is so universally concerned, I mean that of the African and Indian company.

I know some will exclaim against this method, and propose that the business of the army may be first taken into consideration, as of more general concernment to the nation whether it stand or be disbanded. They will not fail to say, that before all other things the king's business (as their style runs) ought to be done. To this I answer, that he who makes a distinction between the business of the king and that of the country, is a true friend to neither. And if it be considered, that the ships of the company are sailed; that Scotland has now a greater venture at sea than at any time since we have been a nation; that the accidents and misfortunes to which an enterprise of this nature is subject, are so many and so various, either by the loss of ships from the ordinary hazards of the sea, or hurricanes; by sickness of the men, who for the most part are neither accustomed to such long voyages, nor to climates so different from their own; by the death of one or more of those to whom the conduct of this affair is principally entrusted; by being disappointed of fresh provisions when those they carry with them are spent; by being attacked at sea or at land, before they have fortified a place for themselves, or a thousand other accidents (for all things are extremely difficult to the first undertakers), I say, if it be considered, that provisions, or the smallest things necessary, falling short but by a few days, have often been the ruin of the greatest undertakings, and chiefly of those of this kind; there cannot be any more urgent affair than that of providing incessantly a supply for the necessities of so many men as are on board those ships, who may be brought under extraordinary sufferings by a delay, whilst our standing forces are living at ease. Especially since the nation has so great a concern in this enterprise, that I may well say all our hopes of ever being any other than a poor and inconsiderable people are embarked with them.

The reputation and power of this nation was formerly very considerable as long as armies were composed of those numerous militias of the barons. Our ancestors have often seen sixty, eighty, or a hundred thousand men under their ensigns, which then might well bear the motto, That none should provoke them unpunished. Since that time, the face of things is quite changed throughout all Europe; and the former militias being altogether decayed, and no good ones anywhere established, every country is obliged to defend itself in time of war, and maintain its reputation by the force of money; that is, by mercenary troops, either of their own or of other countries both by sea and land. But such a vast expense the riches of no country is able to support without a great trade. In this great alteration our case has been singularly bad and unfortunate: for partly through our own fault, and partly by the removal of our kings into another country, this nation, of all those who possess good ports, and lie conveniently for trade and fishing, has been the only part of Europe which did not apply itself to commerce; and possessing a barren country, in less than an age we are sunk to so low a condition as to be despised by all our neighbours, and made incapable to repel an injury, if any should be offered: so that now our motto may be inverted, and all may not only provoke, but safely trample upon us. To recover from such a condition, what would not any people do? What toils would they refuse? To what hazards would they not expose themselves? But if the means by which they are to recover are not only just and honourable, but such as with restoring honour and safety to the nation, may give encouragement to that excellent, though now suppressed and almost extinguished spirit of our people, and gratify every man in the eases and pleasures of life: is it not strange that there should be found men amongst us capable to oppose those things; especially at a time, when, I may say, by no contrivance of any man, but by an unforeseen and unexpected change of the genius of this nation, all their thoughts and inclinations, as if united and directed by a higher power, seem to be turned upon trade, and to conspire together for its advancement, which is the only means to recover us from our present miserable and despicable condition? For hitherto our convenient situation and good harbours, our rich seas and lakes have been unprofitable to us; no care has been taken to set the poor at work; and multitudes of families, for want of employment by trade and manufactures, go yearly out of the kingdom without any intention to return. In such a state and condition of this nation, it seems these men find their account better, than if our country were filled with people and riches, our firths covered with ships, and they should see everywhere the marks of what good government and trade are able to produce.

But I shall be told, that I go upon a mistake; and that no Scotsman is an enemy to the African company: that those who approach his majesty, know most of his mind, and are most entrusted by him in the government of this nation; and such as are influenced by them, would only have the parliament to consider the straits and difficulties his majesty would be put to, if he should in an extraordinary manner encourage this trade, by reason, that being King of England, and Stadt-holder of the United Provinces, our interest in this point may come to interfere with that of those nations. The people of those countries solicit, each in favour of their own companies: will not these men so much as advise the king to distribute impartial justice, and to let every one have the proportionable reward of his industry? Oh, but we have an immunity from customs for many years, which neither the English nor Dutch enjoy. I shall not say, that when the English nation shall come to a perfect knowledge of their interest, they will be con-vinced that riches in Scotland will be beneficial to England, since the seat of the monarchy is there. I need not say that the English and Dutch are free people, and may surely procure for themselves as great advant-ages as Scotland: but that Scotland offered to both nations a share in that advantage which they had obtained for themselves only; and to England an equal share. I know the parliament of England took the thing warmly at first; but when upon due consideration they found that we had not given them the least just ground of offence, but on the contrary, made them the fairest offer we could; it was then let fall, and has not been mentioned in the last session. So that what these gentlemen allege of his majesty's difficulties to satisfy the English in this point is false, unless by the English they mean those who having for many years oppressed the English colonies in America, are afraid that if any settlement should be made in that part of the world by us, under a free constitution, the English planters removing to it, might occasion a strict inquiry into their crimes, and their punishment for them.

I do not hear that the Dutch have presented any memorial to his majesty against our company, and cannot imagine in what terms any such address, either from them, or the English, can run. Should it be, that his majesty ought not to protect us in our just rights and privileges? that he should break the laws, and violate his oath by our destruction? or determine us as the court did the fishing company in King Charles's time, and frustrate this second as well as that first great attempt to make the nation considerable? That there have been underhand deal-ings (though without his majesty's knowledge, as we ought to believe) the affair of Hamburgh does sufficiently demonstrate; and likewise that his majesty's ministers abroad, paid by the Crown of England, are no more to be looked upon as ministers for the Crown of Scotland. Since we are separate kingdoms, and have separate ministers at home, we ought to have separate ministers abroad; especially in an affair wherein we may have a separate interest from England, which must always be in matters of trade, though never so inconsiderable. Neither ought we to have separate ministers only upon the account of trade, but upon all occasions, wherein the honour or interest of the nation is concerned. That we have not had them formerly, since we were under one king with England, was, I suppose, to save charges, and because we trusted to the impartiality of such as we judged to be the ministers of the King of Great Britain: but now we are undeceived, and sure the nation could never have bestowed money better, than in having a minister at the late treaty of peace, who might have obtained the re-establishment of the nation in the privileges they had in France, which was totally neglected: and notwithstanding the great and unproportionable numbers of sea and land soldiers that we were obliged to furnish for the support of the war, yet not one tittle of advantage was procured to us by the peace.

Now these gentlemen, at the same time, would persuade us to pay almost as many forces in time of peace, as we did in time of war; and like Pharaoh's tax-masters would have us make brick without allowing us straw. And all, that these forces, and the regiments, which to the consuming of our people we recruit in Holland, in case of any rupture abroad upon the account of the English or Dutch trade, may be employed in their defence.

To obviate then part of so many shameful things, it is my opinion, that in place of laying a land-tax upon the kingdom for maintaining forces to defend the English and Dutch trade, we should raise one for the carrying on of our own: and (since the nation is so generally concerned in this Indian trade, that the ruin of it, which, God forbid, may very probably draw along with it that of the whole trade of the kingdom, and a perpetual discouragement from ever attempting anything considerable hereafter) that a twelve-months' cess should be levied for the support of it; and that whatsoever may be the product of that money, by the trade of the company, shall go to the easing of the nation from public burdens, whenever they shall make a dividend of clear profit. For it is but reasonable that, since the company has been unjustly hindered of that supply of money which they expected, and might have had from strangers, they should have recourse for redress to the parliament, who if they shall think fit to take such a resolution, the company will be able immediately to procure an advance of money upon the credit of the cess.

It will be also fit, that the company petition the parliament to address his majesty, that the three small frigates, lately built at the expense of this nation, may be appointed for a convoy to the next ships they shall send out.

The parliament having provided for this pressing affair, will (no doubt) proceed to the business of the forces, and to consider whether a standing army shall be kept up in time of peace, as in time of war; for the arguments used to continue them for a year may be improved to keep them up for ever; especially since we have at this time a stronger argument against them than I hope shall ever be alleged hereafter; I mean that of the nation's being exhausted of money by a three years' scarcity next to a famine: but how long this may continue God only knows.

A long and tedious war, which has cost this nation much blood, is at length ended in a peace. Our expense of treasure has been inconsiderable by reason of our poverty through want of trade; yet have we contributed our part, if the smallness of our stock be considered. But in the loss of our people, which is an expense of blood and riches too, we have paid a treble proportion. Seven or eight thousand of our seamen were on board the English fleet, and two or three thousand in that of Holland: we had twenty battalions of foot, and six squadrons of dragoons here and in Flanders. Besides, I am credibly informed, that every fifth man in the English forces was either of this nation, or Scots-Irish, who are a people of the same blood with us. All these, by a modest computation, may amount to thirty thousand men. This I only mention to answer the reproaches of those who vilify us as an inconsiderable people, and set a mean value on the share we have borne in this war. I am unwilling to speak of the returns that have been made to us for our assistance, by refusing to our soldiers the donative given to those who had served no better than they, and by pressing our seamen, contrary to the law of nations. Now though resenting the last of these during the war would have marked us out for disaffection and Jacobitism, yet we ought to hope it may be mentioned at this time without offence. But some will say, that the blessings of peace are so great, that not only the calamities of war, but even affronts and injuries from our neighbours, ought to be forgot and drowned in the joys, which the hopes of ease, tranquillity, and plenty must needs produce. And indeed I should be contented, that all resentments were sacrificed to such charming hopes, if they had any real foundation. But we have a peace, and yet must not reap any benefit by it; a poor country is to

34

maintain almost as many forces as they did in time of war; a nation endeavouring to set up manufactures, and to advance trade, must still see their people consumed, by continuing on foot mercenary forces.

I shall not insist upon the arguments that may be brought against standing forces, nor go about to show how inconsistent they are with liberty. I shall not mention the examples of almost all the nations of Europe, who by keeping up such forces in time of peace are become slaves. This has been fully made out by divers treaties which have been lately published, and are in the hands of most men. Perhaps also it will be said, that I am not to insist upon the point of right in this case, since there is no article in our claim of right to declare the keeping up of a standing army in time of peace, without consent of parliament, to be against law. Yet those who are of that opinion should consider, that the estates of this kingdom have made the keeping up of a standing army, in time of peace, without consent of parliament, an article in the forfaultnre of the late King James. But it seems we must use more modest arguments than such as naturally arise from the hazard our liberty may run, by allowing standing forces, or from any right we have to pretend that it is against the constitution of our government to impose them upon us, and be obliged to bring all our reasons from our necessities and inability to maintain any. Indeed, as this is the most modest, so surely it is the strongest argument; for such forces are not to be maintained, without increasing the poverty of this country, and reducing it at length to utter desolation. It is hard if the charges of a government should be the same in time of peace, or even come near the expense that was perhaps requisite to be made in time of war; such a nation can never hope to be in a flourishing state. Now as our condition will not permit us to keep up these forces, so I can see no reason why we should do it if we could. There is no pretence for them, except only to keep a few wretched Highlanders in order; which might be easily done by a due execution of our old laws made for that purpose, without the help of any fort or garrison. We are at a great distance from any other enemy, and cannot justly fear an invasion from beyond so great a sea as must be passed to come at us. And though during the late war we were sometimes under the apprehensions of such an invasion, yet the enemy was not so imprudent to put it to the hazard.

But some will say, that the late King James has still many partisans in this nation, that we have always been, and still are, a divided people.

and that there are many ill men amongst us: they have also the confidence still to tell us of an invasion upon Scotland by the French King; who, to cover this probable design, has delivered up such vast countries, and places of such great importance. Why do they not also say, that as a man every day after he is born is nearer to his end, so are we every day after the peace nearer to a war? The party of the late King James was always insignificant, and is now become a jest. If the government will encourage good men, they will need no standing forces to secure themselves from the bad. For of what use can any militia be supposed to be, that is not fit to preserve the quiet of a country remote from enemies in time of peace?

Those of the presbyterian persuasion should, I think, be the last of all men to establish an army; for whatever they may promise to themselves, it is certain that either upon his majesty's death, or upon alterations of measures, and changes of dispositions in the minds of the members of future parliaments, it will be always a sure rod for the backs of those who have so many enemies. But men are blind in prosperity, forgetting adversity and the vicissitudes of human affairs. And it were but reasonable that those of that persuasion, who in the late King James's reign made so false a step as was like to have proved fatal to our liberties, should now think of making some amends, and showing that they have profited by their error, and are not (as they express themselves) time-servers.

But to discover the true reason why standing forces are designed to be kept up in this nation in time of peace, we need only look back on the use that was made of them during the late war. For after the reduction of the Highlands they served only for a seminary to the forces of this nation that were with his majesty in Flanders, the best of their men being drawn out yearly for recruiting those forces. This also proves that his majesty knew very well that there was no hazard from the invasions I mentioned before: for if there had been any real danger of that kind, he would not have weakened the forces in this kingdom so considerably. I am very far from disapproving his majesty's conduct in that affair; I do on the contrary highly commend his wisdom in it, and think it to have been the best use that could be made of forces in this country, whilst the war continued. But must we in time of peace be taxed beyond measure to maintain forces, which upon occasion are to serve for the defence of two of the richest nations in the world; nations that have manifested their unwillingness to let us into the least co-partnership with them in trade, from which all our riches, if ever we have any, must arise? This is to load a poor nation with taxes, and to oppress them with soldiers in order to procure plenty and riches to other countries, of which they are not to have the least share. Rich and opulent nations are to enjoy the benefits of the peace, and we are to suffer, that they may enjoy them with security.

Therefore I am of opinion, that since we can expect no advantages from our neighbours or allies, we do ourselves right, by refusing to maintain any standing forces for their behoof, because we need none for our own defence, and that our militia may be sufficient on all occasions where force is necessary. Eighty-four thousand pounds, which is the sum proposed for the yearly maintenance of standing forces, is as much money to us, as two millions five hundred and twenty thousand pounds is to England, since we cannot pretend to above the thirtieth part of their wealth. And yet that nation allows but three hundred and fifty thousand pounds for the forces they keep on foot; of which sum twelve thousand pounds is more than the thirtieth part. If it be said that England allows more for their fleet than for their land forces I answer, it ought to be considered that England with all its riches maintains only five millions and half of people, and that Scotland upon a thirtieth part maintains a million and half. Eighty-four thousand pounds laid out yearly in husbandry, manufactures, and trade may do great things in Scotland, and not only maintain (though in a different way of living) all those officers and soldiers, of which these forces are designed to consist, but also vastly enrich this nation; whereas great numbers of soldiers produce nothing but beggary in any place. People employed in manufactures, husbandry, and trade make consumption as well as soldiers, and their labour and industry is an overplus of wealth to the nation, whilst soldiers consume twice as much as they pay for, and live idle.

It is not the least misfortune of this country, that the younger sons of the nobility and gentry have in all times had their inclinations debauched to an idle, for the most part criminal, and almost always unprofitable sort of life; I mean that of a soldier of fortune. Their talents might have been much better employed in trade and husbandry to the improvement of their country, and increase of their patrimony. Let us begin to come off from such ruinous ways of living; and if we design to carry on a great trade, let us employ men capable to manage it. From all these considerations I say, that the keeping up of any standing forces in time of peace is not only useless, but destructive to the well-being of this nation.

If it be objected, that this would take away even the ordinary guards, I answer, that whilst we had a king residing in Scotland, he had no other guard than forty gentlemen; and now when we have no king amongst us, we must have a squadron of horse and two battalions of foot, with the title of guards. But I would know what guards they are we must keep up. Are they those who yielded up the rank of the nation and dignity of a crown, if it have any pre-eminence above a commonwealth? I am far from pleading for mutiny against a general, or disobedience to a king; but when the meanest officer thinks himself injured in his rank, he demands his pass, and will serve no more; neither is he blamed by any prince for so doing. If the officers of that body would have done as much for the honour of their country, sure they would have merited his majesty's esteem, and deserved rewards from the nation. But how they can pretend to be kept up after an action that our ancestors would have thought to deserve not only breaking, but a decimation to precede it, I cannot imagine. I know there are many brave gentlemen among them who were much grieved at the thing, but they had a bad example from the then commanding officer; and it is to be feared that his advancement to the place of the greatest military trust and importance in the kingdom, may by his majesty's enemies be imputed to that action.

But after all we are told, that if we will keep up standing forces we shall have an act of habeas corpus. This would be a wise bargain: here is a price for our liberty; sure we may expect an immense sum, and a security without exception. No, no, but you shall have an act of parliament for the freedom of your persons, though there be never so many standing forces in the kingdom; that is, we shall have the law on our side, and another shall have the force, and then let nature work. If there be no danger that standing forces should violate the law, there is no danger from them.

There is no pretence to speak of a cess or land-tax for maintaining forces, before the business of the army be taken into consideration; and one would think, if the army be disbanded, it should not be mentioned at all. Yet it is certain that such men as would recommend themselves by a pretended loyalty, will not fail to tell us, that we ought to be at the least as liberal to his present majesty, who has redeemed us from popery and slavery, as we were to King James, who would have brought us under both: and though they now pretend that a cess for life will not be so much as mentioned in the approaching session, we know very well their conduct in that affair will be regulated

38

upon the disposition they find in the parliament to grant or refuse it; and that if they conceive any hopes of obtaining so considerable a jewel to the crown, they will be sure to bring in that affair when least expected.

The giving his majesty a land-tax during life, and so great a one as that granted to the late King James, with the revenue already settled on him for the same term, makes it impossible for the subject to give more, and consequently is of all those affairs that can come before any parliament the greatest, and of the highest importance; since it tends to the making parliaments less necessary, and consequently to the abolishing them, with the ancient constitution of government in this nation.

Those who have the honour to advise his present majesty, if they be true lovers of the monarchy, ought to have a care of treading in the former footsteps, and above all shun to advise him to desire those things of the parliament which King James desired and obtained. It were their duty by all means to endeavour a fair understanding and a continual good correspondence between king and people, which certainly is the only true support of monarchy. Now there are no occasions of entertaining and increasing that confidence, and those mutual good offices that should, like regular tides, ebb and flow between king and people, greater than those of parliaments. Endeavours to take away the frequency of parliaments are endeavours to take away those frequent good offices between king and people. The king stands in need of money, the people of good laws, which their representatives and his great council offer to him, that they may have his sanction, and that he may provide for their due execution. Money may be given at once, for a long time, or for ever; but good laws cannot be so enacted, the occasion and necessity of them discovering itself only from time to time: and if the one go without the other, the mutual good offices, and consequently the mutual confidence between king and people ceases.

It may be farther considered, that the king has the power of calling parliaments; and that by giving him for life all that we can give, we shall make parliaments unnecessary to him. If any man suggest that it is a crime to suspect that so good and just a prince as his present majesty is, will not always do what is for the good of his people, I answer, that I have all the deference, respect, and esteem for his majesty that any subject ought to have; but it were a fulsome piece of flattery for any man to say that he cannot be influenced by bad counsel, or that he is not subject to those frailties of mistake and prejudice, from

39

which no mortal was ever free, and princes always most subject to through the suggestions and bad offices of men about them.

But let us suppose that his present majesty will never make the least bad use of this tax, who shall secure us his successor will not? If it be said that it is only for his present majesty this tax is desired, and that it is in the power of the parliament to refuse it to the successor, I say, with what probability will it, and with what face can it be refused to him? These men desire it for his present majesty because King James had it, though he made bad use of it; the successor shall desire it because his present majesty had it, and made good use of it; I think his argument is stronger. So that though this be said to be only for the life of his present majesty, yet upon the matter it is for ever. And then I need not tell you the consequence, our parliaments shall be abolished, our kings shall become tyrants, and we, of subjects, slaves.

But if we look more nearly into this demand, I doubt not it will appear very gross. During the late war, land-taxes were only demanded from year to year, and we gave them cheerfully, in hopes that a few years would put an end to that charge. When we had undoubted reasons to believe there would be a peace, they were demanded to be given for two years; and now God has blessed us with it, if they be demanded during his majesty's life, will not this look as if we were to have a standing army during the same time?

A land-tax during his majesty's life is a French *taille* for that time. And we ought not to forget that we are beginning, to the great advantage of the nation, to make some small progress in trade; but if it be not encouraged, and much more if it be nipped in the bud, there is an end of all our hopes. One of the greatest things in trade is to encourage exportation; and it is known that the greatest commodity of this kingdom is corn: if there be a land-tax on those whose chief riches consist in corn, they cannot sell so cheap to the merchant that he can make any profit by exporting it.

As for the arguments of those who are for this tax, I need answer none of them; they are, to save the trouble and expense of frequent parliaments; and because the nation did trust King James with this tax, who made bad use of it (a modest and a sensible argument!) are they not afraid it should be said, that those who advise the King to ask the same trust King James had, may advise him likewise to the same things, for which King James demanded it? Sure I am, that many who plead for this now are the same persons who did the like for King James: and as for the expense occasioned by frequent parliaments, I believe there is neither shire nor borough but will find persons very willing to represent them, without putting them to any charge. I know it is commonly said in this kingdom that parliaments do more hurt than good; but it is because they are never called unless to impose money: will it mend the matter to lay on at once, and for life, as much as the nation is able to pay? We were getting some good laws for our money, but then we shall be excluded from that benefit.

In a word, our forefathers had two securities for their liberties and properties, they had both the sword and the purse: the sword anciently was in the hand of the subject, because the armies then were composed of the vassals who depended on the barons. That security is gone; shall we throw the other after it, and thereby, I may very well say, dissolve the constitution, and the monarchy? For a government is not only a tyranny, when tyrannically exercised; but also when there is no sufficient caution in the constitution that it may not be exercised tyrannically.

When the parliament has put an end to the affairs before-mentioned, it were to be wished that this being the first session since the conclusion of the peace, and after so long a war, they would pass some act to ease the minds, and take away the fears and apprehensions of many men who are still obnoxious to the law, of whom the greater part are abroad; and all of them both at home and abroad, for want of an act of indemnity, made desperate, and only fitted to involve others in the same uneasy and distracting circumstances under which they themselves live. But acts of indemnity are the worst and most pernicious of all laws to the well-being of any government, unless the most notorious offenders be first punished; and in such cases only encouragements to new transgressions, destroying the real security of all government, and effect of all laws, by giving an entire impunity to the attempts against both. So that there seems to be an absolute necessity, both of making an example of the notorious enemies to the liberties of this country, and giving a general pardon to the rest; if we will either secure the government for the future from endeavours to introduce arbitrary power, cut up the party of the late King James by the roots, or quiet the minds of the people, and remove the animosities that may remain in a nation wherein two or more parties have been inflamed against each other, to the ruin of the public liberty, and extinguish the memory of those factions for ever.

When it is confessed and acknowledged that there have been bold attempts and treacherous practices to destroy the religion, overturn the constitution of government, and suppress the liberty of a nation, and yet no example made of the advisers, and those who have been eminently subservient to such designs; such a people has as much laid the foundation of their own ruin, as if they had declared that those who shall hereafter engage themselves in the like attempts, need fear no punishment. Upon a revolution followed by a war, circumstances of affairs may be such that till the war be at an end, it is not fit to punish great offenders. But there was no reason, nor any well-grounded political consideration, why immediately upon the late revolution, the most notorious of those offenders should not have been punished; by which means we should have been delivered from our worst men, who have since been very bad instruments in affairs, and have terrified the rest by their example: we might then have quieted the minds of the people by an indemnity; brought the nation to a settlement, and prevented the war which ensued in this country. Yet (because in matters of prudence men are of different sentiments) though it should be granted, that during the war it was not fit to make any examples, what pretence can there be now of exempting from punishment those who have been notoriously criminal, both under the late reigns, and under this? which when it is done, what conjuncture of time can be so proper for applying the healing remedy of an act of indemnity and oblivion to the rest, as the present, by reason of the peace?

Before the revolution, the court had been in a formed conspiracy against the religion and liberties of this nation; nor was there any art to introduce arbitrary power, or subvert our religion, for which the late reigns wanted willing instruments; and many endeavoured to signalize themselves in the ruin of their country. Yet no man has been made an example, to deter others from the like crimes. It will I know be thought hard to mention the punishing of offences committed so many years ago, when many of the offenders are dead; and some men will judge it fitter to bury all in a general act of oblivion. To this I answer, that having been highly to blame for neglecting hitherto to punish the enemies of our liberty, this ought to oblige us the rather to make an example of those who are still living. And to convince us of this necessity, we need only to consider what crimes those men would not have punished, nor the least example made of any that have been guilty of them; and whether the suffering them to pass unpunished will not bring a guilt upon the nation which may not easily be expiated. Public and private injuries are of a very different nature; and though we are commanded to forgive the last, yet those who have power and right, are required, under the greatest penalties, to punish the other, especially where the crimes are enormous. But if the parliament should follow the advice of those men, they are not to punish any violent proceedings, illegal and arbitrary imprisonments, fines, banishments, and murders under pretext of law, that were set on foot, encouraged, and committed by those evil counsellors mentioned in his majesty's declaration, in order to alter the religion and government of this nation, and in place of them to introduce popery and slavery. They are not to punish those who to recommend themselves to the late kings, by their interest, power, and credit in the parliament, got to be enacted most cruel and unchristian laws, for persecuting a great part of this nation upon the account of their religious opinions, which they could not quit without violating their consciences: they are not to punish those privy counsellors who went further than those very laws would allow them, in a thousand arbitrary and illegal proceedings, issuing out orders to invade such as dissented from them only in religious matters, with an army composed for the most part of barbarous Highlanders, who hunted them from hill to hill, to force them to take arms, that they might have a pretext to destroy them utterly. They are not to punish those who gave orders to impose illegal and unwarrantable oaths upon all persons, even on silly women that might be found travelling in the ordinary road, and to shoot them immediately dead, if they should refuse the same. Nor are they to punish those who put them in execution. Do presbyterians in particular imagine, that if they neglect their duty in punishing these men, they will avoid the guilt of the innocent blood shed in those times? Are such things to be pardoned as private injuries? The making our courts of justice, particularly that of the session, to be the instruments of subjecting all men to arbitrary power, are things to be passed over in silence, and no account to be taken of them. Those who advised and drew a proclamation, declaring the late King James his absolute power in express terms, are not to be questioned for it. If the parliament pass over these things without making any example of the offenders, they make a precedent for abolishing the punishment of all enormous crimes for ever, since there never can be greater than these. Shall there be no examples made of criminals for enormities of such a general influence and concernment, in a nation where a poor man for stealing a little food, is for example's sake (let what I say be considered is for example's sake) punished with death? If there can be no stop put to the least of crimes, but by the punishment of some of those that are guilty; can

43

there be any remedy against the abettors of arbitrary power, if no example be made of them? Can that government be said to be secure, where there is no punishment, but rewards for conspiracies against its constitution? It is true that it may be fit to overlook some crimes, wherein extraordinary numbers of men are concerned, but not extraordinary crimes, nor the most guilty of the criminals.

It was thought fit to forbear the punishment of the evil counsellors mentioned in his majesty's declaration for some time; that forbearance has lasted to this day; and we have so little hopes of seeing any discouragement put upon those who shall promote arbitrary government in time to come, by an exemplary punishment of the most notorious offenders under the late reigns, that notwithstanding many new provocations, and reiterated treasons under this, they have not only hitherto escaped punishment, but have been also encouraged. For not long after the revolution, the most considerable of them (I do not speak of those who took arms) entered into new conspiracies against their country, to betray it again to the late King James, and took the oaths to this King, that they might have the better opportunity to bring back the other. Yet after all this his majesty was advised to put some of them into the most important places of trust in the kingdom. What are we then to expect, if we shall not now proceed to make some examples, but that they, and men of the like principles, will insinuate themselves into all the places of trust; and have the power as well as the will to throw us into prisons, and by their pernicious counsels to betray his present majesty into the same misfortunes that were brought upon the late King? Is it not enough, that the punishment of those who endeavoured to enslave us under the late reigns has been delayed till now? Because they have renewed the same practices under this, must it still be delayed, to the end that (as they have already done in the affair of Glencoe) they may continue to give his majesty the same bad counsel with which the late kings were poisoned? Now, to pardon them we have this encouragement, that having passed over former crimes, we embolden them to commit new, and to give fresh wounds to that country which has already so often bled under their hands.

When the greatest offenders are punished, an act of indemnity will be as necessary to the well-being of this nation as peace itself, since there can be no ease or quiet without it. But so little hopes have we of this, that whilst the evil counsellors, against whom his majesty did so justly declare, live at ease, an act (as we are told) is to be brought into the parliament for banishing during pleasure many thousands of inconsiderable people who cannot be charged with crimes any way comparable to theirs; and some of them free of the least appearance of any. What construction would the advisers of these things have even those who are best affected to the government put upon them? One might reasonably think that such things may be fit to keep up the party of the late King James, and fright the nation into a belief of the necessity of continuing a standing army, that they may be fit to lead men of estates, or those who have anything to lose, into snares both at home and abroad (particularly in France, where the late King James is still suffered) by pretending correspondence or conversation with such as may be obnoxious to the law: but no man can suspect the worst of counsellors of such designs. And therefore I confess I am at a stand; for such vast numbers of people were never yet banished for crimes of state: nor does the multitude ever suffer for them, except only in barbarous countries. If it be said that ill men may have designs against his majesty's life, and therefore ought to be banished, I answer, nothing is more likely to draw on such a mischief than extraordinary severities used against them. For nothing does so much fit a man for such an attempt as despair; against which no distance of place can long protect.

My opinion therefore is that an act of indemnity (excepting only assassins and other notorious criminals, whom we cannot at present reach) is more suitable to our present condition than an act of banishment: and that to procure the nation so great a blessing, the parliament should proceed, without delay, to the punishing of the greatest criminals, both of this and the last reigns without which an oblivion will be one of the greatest injuries that can be done to us.

I shall only add, that there is ground to believe some men will endeavour to persuade the parliament to take this affair into consideration before all others; because it was the first thing done in the last sesssion of the English parliament; and the bill having passed there almost without debate, they will make use of that as an argument why it should do so here. What the considerations were which moved that parliament to do so, I will not presume to determine, neither is it my business; circumstances of affairs may be different in different nations: sure I am, that in this particular they are different, that a greater number of men, in proportion to the people in each nation, will fall under uneasy circumstances by such an act in Scotland, than has been found to have done in England.

THE SECOND
DISCOURSE
CONCERNING THE
AFFAIRS OF SCOTLAND;
WRITTEN IN THE YEAR 1698

The affairs of which I have spoken in the preceding discourse are such as the present conjuncture makes a proper subject for the approaching session of parliament: but there are many other things which require no less their care, if the urgent and pressing distresses of the nation be considered. I shall therefore with all due respect to the parliament offer my opinion concerning two, which I presume to be of that nature.

The first thing which I humbly and earnestly propose to that honourable court is, that they would take into their consideration the condition of so many thousands of our people who are at this day dying for want of bread. And to persuade them seriously to apply themselves to so indispensable a duty, they have all the inducements which those most powerful emotions of the soul, terror and compassion, can produce. Because from unwholesome food diseases are so multiplied among the poor people, that if some course be not taken, this famine may very probably be followed by a plague; and then what man is there even of those who sit in parliament that can be sure he shall escape? And what man is there in this nation, if he have any compassion, who must not grudge himself every nice bit and every delicate morsel he puts in his mouth, when he considers that so many are already dead, and so many at that minute struggling with death, not for want of bread but of grains, which I am credibly informed have been eaten by some families, even during the preceding years of scarcity. And must not every unnecessary branch of our expense, or the least finery in our houses, clothes, or equipage, reproach us with our barbarity, so long as people born with natural endowments, perhaps not inferior to our own, and fellow citizens, perish for want of things absolutely necessary to life?

But not to insist any more upon the representation of so great a calamity, which if drawn in proper colours, and only according to the precise truth of things, must cast the minds of all honest men into those convulsions which ought necessarily to be composed before they can calmly consider of a remedy; and because the particulars of this great distress are sufficiently known to all, I shall proceed to say, that though perhaps upon the great want of bread, occasioned by the continued bad seasons of this and the three preceding years, the evil be greater and more pressing than at any time in our days, yet there have always been in Scotland such numbers of poor, as by no regulations could ever be orderly provided for; and this country has always swarmed with such numbers of idle vagabonds, as no laws could ever restrain. And indeed when I considered the many excellent laws enacted by former parliaments for setting the poor to work, particularly those in the time of King James the sixth, with the clauses for putting them in execution, which to me seemed such as could not miss of the end, and yet that nothing was obtained by them, I was amazed, and began to think upon the case of other nations in this particular, persuaded that there was some strange hidden root of this evil which could not be well discovered, unless by observing the conduct of other governments. But upon reflection I found them all subject to the same inconveniences, and that in all the countries of Europe there were great numbers of poor, except in Holland, which I knew to proceed from their having the greatest share in the trade of the world. But this not being a remedy for every country, since all cannot pretend to so great a part in trade, and that two or three nations are able to manage the whole commerce of Europe; yet there being a necessity that the poor should everywhere be provided for, unless we will acknowledge the deficiency of all government in that particular, and finding no remedy in the laws or customs of any of the present governments, I began to consider what might be the conduct of the wise ancients in that affair. And my curiosity was increased, when upon reflection I could not call to mind that any ancient author had so much as mentioned such a thing, as great numbers of poor in any country.

At length I found the original of that multitude of beggars which now oppress the world, to have proceeded from churchmen, who (never failing to confound things spiritual with temporal, and consequently all good order and good government, either through mistake or design) upon the first public establishment of the Christian religion,

47

recommended nothing more to masters, in order to the salvation of their souls, than the setting such of their slaves at liberty as would embrace the Christian faith, though our Saviour and his apostles had been so far from making use of any temporal advantages to persuade eternal truths, and so far from invading any man's property, by promising him heaven for it, that the apostle Paul says expressly, 'In whatever condition of life every one is called to the Christian faith, in that let him remain. Art thou called being a slave? Be not concerned for thy condition; but even though thou mightest be free, choose to continue in it. For he who is called whilst a slave, becomes the freeman of the Lord; and likewise he that is called whilst a freeman, becomes the slave of Christ, who has paid a price for you, that you might not be the slaves of men. Let every one therefore, brethren, in whatever condition he is called, in that remain, in the fear of God.' That the interpretation I put upon this passage, different from our translation, is the true meaning of the apostle, not only the authority of the Greek fathers, and genuine signification of the Greek particles, but the whole context, chiefly the first and last words (which seem to be repeated to enforce and determine such a meaning) clearly demonstrate. And the reason why he recommends to them rather to continue slaves (if they have embraced the Christian faith in that condition) seems to be that it might appear they did not embrace it for any worldly advantage, as well as to destroy a doctrine which even in his days began to be preached, that slavery was inconsistent with the Christian religion; since such a doctrine would have been a great stop to the progress of it. What the apostle means by saying, we ought not to be the slaves of men, I shall show hereafter.

This disorder of giving liberty to great numbers of slaves upon their profession of Christianity, grew to such a height, even in the time of Constantine the great, that the cities of the empire found themselves burdened with an infinite number of men, who had no other estate but their liberty, of whom the greatest part would not work, and the rest had been bred to no profession. This obliged Constantine to make edicts in favour of beggars; and from that time at the request of the bishops, hospitals, and alms-houses, not formerly known in the world, began to be established. But upon the rise of the Mahometan religion, which was chiefly advanced by giving liberty to all their slaves, the Christians were so molested by the continual rebellion of theirs, that they were at length forced to give liberty to them all; which it seems the churchmen then looked upon as a thing necessary to preserve the Christian religion, since in many of the writings, by which masters gave freedom to their slaves, it is expressly said, they did so, to save their own souls.

This is the rise of that great mischief, under which, to the undoing of the poor, all the nations of Europe have ever since groaned. Because in ancient times, so long as a man was the riches and part of the possession of another, every man was provided for in meat, clothes, and lodging; and not only he, but (in order to increase that riches) his wife and children also: whereas provisions by hospitals, alms-houses, and the contributions of churches or parishes have by experience been found to increase the numbers of those that live by them. And the liberty every idle and lazy person has of burdening the society in which he lives, with his maintenance, has increased their numbers to the weakening and impoverishing of it: for he needs only to say that he cannot get work, and then he must be maintained by charity. And as I have shown before, no nation except one only (which is in extraordinary circumstances) does provide by public work-houses for their poor: the reason of which seems to be, that public work-houses for such vast numbers of people are impracticable except in those places where (besides a vast trade to vend the manufactured goods) there is an extraordinary police, and that though the Hollanders by reason of the steadiness of their temper, as well as of their government (being a commonwealth) may be constant to their methods of providing for the poor; yet in a nation, and under a government like that of France, though vast public work-houses may be for a while kept in order, it will not be long before they fall into confusion and ruin. And indeed (next to Plato's republic, which chiefly consists in making the whole society live in common) there is nothing more impracticable than to provide for so great a part of every nation by public work-houses. Whereas when such an economy comes under the inspection of every master of a family, and that he himself is to reap the profit of the right management; the thing not only turns to a far better account, but by reason of his power to sell those workmen to others who may have use for them, when he himself has a mind to alter his course of life, the profit is permanent to the society; nor can such an economy or any such management ever fall into confusion.

I doubt not, that what I have said will meet, not only with all the misconstruction and obloquy, but all the disdain, fury, and out-cries, of which either ignorant magistrates, or proud, lazy, and miserable people are capable. Would I bring back slavery into the world? Shall men of immortal souls, and by nature equal to any, be sold as beasts? Shall they and their posterity be for ever subjected to the most miserable of all conditions; the inhuman barbarity of masters, who may beat, mutilate, torture, starve, or kill so great a number of mankind at pleasure? Shall the far greater part of the commonwealth be slaves, not that the rest may be free, but tyrants over them? With what face can we oppose the tyranny of princes, and recommend such opposition as the highest virtue, if we make ourselves tyrants over the greatest part of mankind? Can any man, from whom such a thing has once escaped, ever offer to speak for liberty? But they must pardon me if I tell them, that I regard not names, but things; and that the misapplication of names has confounded everything. We are told there is not a slave in France; that when a slave sets his foot upon French ground, he becomes immediately free: and I say, that there is not a freeman in France, because the king takes away any part of any man's property at his pleasure; and that, let him do what he will to any man, there is no remedy. The Turks tell us, there are no slaves among them, except Jews, Moors, or Christians; and who is there that knows not, they are all slaves to the grand Seignior, and have no remedy against his will? A slave properly is one who is absolutely subjected to the will of another man without any remedy: and not one that is only subjected under certain limitations, and upon certain accounts necessary for the good of the commonwealth, though such a one may go under that name. And the confounding these two conditions of men by a name common to both, has in my opinion been none of the least hardships put upon those who ought to be named servants. We are all subjected to the laws; and the easier or harder conditions imposed by them upon the several ranks of men in any soceity, make not the distinction that is between a freeman and a slave.

So that the condition of slaves among the ancients will upon serious consideration appear to be only a better provision in their governments than any we have, that no man might want the necessities of life, nor any person able to work be burdensome to the commonwealth. And they wisely judged of the inconveniences that befall the most part of poor people, when they are all abandoned to their own conduct. I know that these two conditions of men were confounded under the same name, as well by the ancients as they are by us; but the reason was, that having often taken in war the subjects of absolute monarchs, they thought they did them no wrong if they did not better their condition: and as in some of their governments the condition of slaves was under a worse regulation than in others, so in some of them it differed very little, if at all, from the condition of such a slave as I have defined. But I do not approve, and therefore will not go about to defend any of those bad and cruel regulations about slaves. And because it would be tedious and needless to pursue the various conditions of them in several ages and governments, it shall be enough for me to explain under what conditions they might be both good and useful, as well as I think they are necessary in a well-regulated government.

First then, their masters should not have power over their lives, but the life of the master should go for the life of the servant. The master should have no power to mutilate or torture him; that in such cases the servant should not only have his freedom (which alone would make him burdensome to the public) but a sufficient yearly pension so long as he should live from his said master. That he, his wife, and children should be provided for in clothes, diet, and lodging. That they should be taught the principles of morality and religion; to read, and be allowed the use of certain books: that they should not work upon Sundays, and be allowed to go to church: that in everything, except their duty as servants, they should not be under the will of their masters, but the protection of the law: that when these servants grow old, and are no more useful to their masters (lest upon that account they should be ill-used) hospitals should be provided for them by the public: that if for their good and faithful service, any master give them their freedom, he should be obliged to give them likewise wherewithal to subsist, or put them in a way of living without being troublesome to the commonwealth: that they should wear no habit or mark to distinguish them from hired servants: that any man should be punished who gives them the opprobrious name of slave. So, except it were that they could possess nothing, and might be sold, which really would be but an alienation of their service without their consent, they would live in a much more comfortable condition (wanting nothing necessary for life) than those who having a power to possess all things, are very often in want of everything, to such a degree, that many thousands of them come to starve for hunger.

It will be said, that notwithstanding all these regulations, they may be most barbarously used by their masters, either by beating them outrageously, making them work beyond measure, suffer cold or hunger, or neglecting them in their sickness. I answer, that as long as the servant is of an age not unfit for work, all these things are against the interest of the master: that the most brutal man will not use his beast ill only out of a humour; and that if such inconveniences do sometimes fall out, it proceeds, for the most part, from the perverseness of the servant: that all inconveniences cannot be obviated by any government; that we must choose the least; and that to prevent them in the best manner possible, a particular magistrate might be instituted for that end.

The condition of such a servant is to be esteemed free; because in the most essential things he is only subject to the laws, and not to the will of his master, who can neither take away his life, mutilate, torture, or restrain him from the comforts of wife and children: but on the other hand, for the service he does, is obliged to ease him of the inconveniences of marriage, by providing for him, his wife, and children, clothes, food, and lodging: and the condition of a bashaw, or great lord, under arbitrary government (who for the sake, and from a necessity of what they call government, has joined to the quality of a slave the office of a tyrant, and imagines himself a man of quality, if not a little prince, by such pre-eminence) is altogether slavish; since he is under the protection of no law, no not so much as to his life, or the honour of his wife and children; and is subjected to stronger temptations than any man, of being a slave to men in St. Paul's sense, which is a worse sort of slavery than any I have yet mentioned. That is of being subservient to, and an instrument of the lusts of his master the tyrant: since if he refuse slavishly to obey, he must lose his office, and perhaps his life. And indeed men of all ranks living under arbitrary government (so much preached and recommended by the far greater part of churchmen) being really under the protection of no law (whatever may be pretended) are not only slaves, as I have defined before, but by having no other certain remedy in anything against the lust and passions of their superiors, except suffering or compliance, lie under the most violent temptations of being slaves in the worst sense, and of the only sort that is inconsistent with the Christian religion. A condition (whatever men may imagine) so much more miserable than that of servants protected by the laws in all things necessary for the subsistence of them and their posterity, that there is no comparison.

I shall now proceed to the great advantages the ancients received from this sort of servants. By thus providing for their poor, and making every man useful to the commonwealth, they were not only able to perform those great and stupendous public works, highways, aqueducts, common-shores, walls of cities, seaports, bridges, monuments for the dead, temples, amphitheatres, theatres, places for all manner of exercises and education, baths, courts of justice, market-places, public walks, and other magnificent works for the use and conveniency of the public, with which Egypt, Asia, Greece, Italy and other countries were filled; and to adorn them with stately pillars and obelisks, curious statues, most exquisite sculpture and painting: but every particular man might indulge himself in any kind of finery and magnificence; not only because he had slaves to perform it according to his fancy, but because all the poor being provided for, there could be no crime in making unnecessary expenses, which are always contrary, not only to Christian charity, but common humanity, as long as any poor man wants bread. For though we think that in making those expenses, we employ the poor; and that in building costly houses, and furnishing them, making fine gardens, rich stuffs, laces and embroideries for apparel, the poor are set to work; yet so long as all the poor are not provided for (though a man cannot reproach himself in particular why it is not done) and that there is any poor family in a starving condition, it is against common humanity (and no doubt would have been judged to be so by the ancients) for any man to indulge himself in things unnecessary, when others want what is absolutely necessary for life, especially since the furnishing of those things to them does employ workmen as well as our unnecessary expenses. So that the ancients, without giving the least check to a tender compassion for the necessities of others (a virtue so natural to great minds, so nicely to be preserved and cherished) might not only adorn their public buildings with all the refinements of art, but likewise beautify their private houses, villas, and gardens with the greatest curiosity. But we by persisting in the like, and other unnecessary expenses, while all the poor are not provided for (example, vanity, and the love of pleasure, being predominant in us) have not only effaced all the vestiges of Christian charity, but banished natural compassion from amongst us, that without remorse we might continue in them.

This explains to us by what means so much virtue and simplicity of manners could subsist in the cities of Greece, and the lesser Asia, in the midst of so great curiosity and refinement in the arts of magnificence and ornament. For in ancient times great riches, and consequently bad arts to acquire them, were not necessary for those things; because if a man possessed a moderate number of slaves, he might choose to employ them in any sort of magnificence, either private or public, for use or ornament, as he thought fit, whilst he himself lived in the greatest simplicity, having neither coaches nor horses to carry him, as in triumph, through the city; nor a family in most things composed like that of a prince, and a multitude of idle servants to consume his estate. Women were not then intolerably expensive, but wholly employed in the care of domestic affairs. Neither did the furniture of their houses amount to such vast sums as with us, but was for the most part wrought by their slaves.

Another advantage which the ancients had by this sort of servants, was, that they were not under that uneasiness, and unspeakable vexation which we suffer by our hired servants, who are never bred to be good for anything, though most of the slaves amongst the ancients were. And though we bestow the greatest pains or cost to educate one of them from his youth, upon the least cross word he leaves us. So that it is more than probable this sort of servants growing every day worse, the unspeakable trouble arising from them, without any other consideration, will force the world to return to the former.

Among the ancients, any master who had the least judgment or discretion, was served with emulation by all his slaves, that those who best performed their duty might obtain their liberty from him. A slave, though furnished with everything necessary, yet possessing nothing, had no temptation to cheat his master; whereas a hired servant, whilst he remains unmarried, will cheat his master of what may be a stock to him when married; and if after his marriage he continue to serve his master, he will be sure to cheat him much more. When the ancients gave freedom to a slave, they were obliged to give him wherewithal to subsist, or to put him into a way of living. And how well and faithfully they were served by those they had made free (whom from a long experience of their probity and capacity, they often made stewards of their estates) all ancient history does testify. Now, we having no regular way to enable a servant to provide sufficient maintenance for his family, when he becomes independent on his master, his bare wages (out of which he is for the most part to provide himself with many necessaries for daily use) not being enough for that purpose, and no way left but to cheat his master, we ought not to expect any probity or fidelity in our servants, because, for want of order in this point, we subject them to such strong temptation.

I might insist upon many other advantages the ancients had in the way they were served, if to persuade the expedient I propose, I were not to make use of stronger arguments than such as can be drawn from any advantages; I mean those of necessity.

There are at this day in Scotland (besides a great many poor families very meanly provided for by the church-boxes, with others, who by living upon bad food fall into various diseases) two hundred thousand people begging from door to door. These are not only no way advantageous, but a very grievous burden to so poor a country. And though the number of them be perhaps double to what it was formerly, by reason of this present great distress, yet in all times there have been about one hundred thousand of those vagabonds, who have lived without any regard or subjection either to the laws of the land, or even those of God and nature; fathers incestuously accompanying with their own daughters, the son with the mother, and the brother with the sister. No magistrate could ever discover or be informed which way one in a hundred of these wretches died, or that ever they were baptized. Many murders have been discovered among them; and they are not only a most unspeakable oppression to poor tenants (who if they give not bread, or some kind of provision to perhaps forty such villains in one day, are sure to be insulted by them) but they rob many poor people who live in houses distant from any neighbourhood. In years of plenty many thousands of them meet together in the mountains, where they feast and riot for many days; and at country weddings, markets, burials, and other the like public occasions, they are to be seen both men and women perpetually drunk, cursing, blaspheming, and fighting together.

These are such outrageous disorders, that it were better for the nation they were sold to the galleys or West Indies, than that they should continue any longer to be a burden and curse upon us. But numbers of people being great riches, every government is to blame that makes not a right use of them. The wholesomeness of our air, and healthfulness of our climate, affords us great numbers of people, which in so poor a country can never be all maintained by manufactures, or public work-houses, or any other way, but that which I have mentioned.

And to show that former parliaments struggling with this, otherwise insuperable, difficulty, have by the nature of the thing been as it were forced upon remedies tending towards what I have proposed: by an act of parliament in the year 1579, any subject of sufficient estate is allowed to take the child of any beggar, and educate him for his service, which child is obliged to serve such a master for a certain term of years; and that term of years extended by another act made in the year 1597, for life. So that here is a great advance towards my proposition; but either from some mistake about Christian or civil liberty, they did not proceed to consider the necessity of continuing that service in the children of such servants, and giving their masters a power of alienating that service to whom they should think fit. The reason for the first of these is, that being married in that sort of service, their masters must of necessity maintain their wife and children, and so ought to have the same right to the service of the children as of the father. And the reason for the power of alienation is, that no man is sure of continuing always in one sort of employment; and having educated a great many such children when he was in an employment that required many servants, if afterwards he should be obliged to quit it for one that required few or none, he could not without great injustice be deprived of the power of alienating their service to any other man, in order to reimburse to himself the money he had bestowed upon them; especially since the setting them at liberty would only bring a great burden on the public.

Now what I would propose upon the whole matter is, that for some present remedy of so great a mischief, every man of a certain estate in this nation should be obliged to take a proportionable number of those vagabonds, and either employ them in hedging and ditching his grounds, or any other sort of work in town and country; or if they happen to be children and young, that he should educate them in the knowledge of some mechanical art, that so every man of estate might have a little manufacture at home which might maintain those servants, and bring great profit to the master, as they did to the ancients, whose revenue by the manufactures of such servants was much more considerable than that of their lands. Hospitals and alms-houses ought to be provided for the sick, lame, and decrepit, either by rectifying old foundations or instituting new. And for example and terror three or four hundred of the most notorious of those villains which we call jockys, might be presented by the government to the state of Venice, to serve in their galleys against the common enemy of Christendom.

But these things, when once resolved, must be executed with great address, diligence, and severity; for that sort of people is so desperately wicked, such enemies of all work and labour, and, which is yet more amazing, so proud, in esteeming their own condition above that which they will be sure to call slavery; that unless prevented by the utmost industry and diligence, upon the first publication of any orders necessary for putting in execution such a design, they will rather die with hunger in caves and dens, and murder their young children, than appear abroad to have them and themselves taken into such a kind of service. And the Highlands are such a vast and unsearchable retreat for them, that if strict and severe order be not taken to prevent it, upon such an occasion these vagabonds will only rob as much food as they can out of the low-country, and retire to live upon it in those mountains, or run into England till they think the storm of our resolutions is over, which in all former times they have seen to be vain.

Nor indeed can there be a thorough reformation in this affair, so long as the one half of our country, in extent of ground, is possessed by a people who are all gentlemen only because they will not work; and who in everything are more contemptible than the vilest slaves, except that they always carry arms, because for the most part they live upon robbery. This part of the country being an inexhaustible source of beggars, has always broke all our measures relating to them. And it were to be wished that the government would think fit to transplant that handful of people, and their masters (who have always disturbed our peace) into the low-country, and people the Highlands from hence, rather than they should continue to be a perpetual occasion of mischief to us. It is in vain to say, that whatever people are planted in those mountains, they will quickly turn as savage, and as great beggars as the present inhabitants; for the mountains of the Alps are greater, more desert, and more condemned to snows that those of the Highlands of Scotland, which are everywhere cut by friths and lakes, the the richest in fishing of any in the world, affording great conveniences for transportation of timber and any other goods; and yet the Alps which have no such advantages are inhabited everywhere by a civilized, industrious, honest, and peaceable people: but they had no lords to hinder them from being civilized, to discourage industry, encourage thieving, and to keep them beggars that they might be the more dependent; or when they had any that oppressed them, as in that part of the mountains that belongs to the Swiss, they knocked them on the head.

Let us now compare the condition of our present vagabonds with that of servants under the conditions which I have proposed, and we shall see the one living under no law of God, man, or nature, polluted with all manner of abominations; and though in so little expectation of the good things of another life, yet in the worst condition of this, and sometimes starved to death in time of extraordinary want. The other, though sometimes they may fall under a severe master (who nevertheless may neither kill, mutilate, nor torture them, and may be likewise restrained from using them very ill by the magistrate I mentioned) are always sure to have food, clothes, and lodging; and have this advantage above other men, that without any care or pains taken by them, these necessaries are likewise secured to their wives and children. They are provided for in sickness, their children are educated, and all of them under all the inducements, encouragements, and obligations possible to live quiet, innocent, and virtuous lives. They may also hope, if they show an extraordinary affection, care, and fidelity in the service of their master, that not only they and their families shall have their entire freedom, but a competency to live, and perhaps the estate of the master entrusted to their care. Now if we will consider the advantages to the nation by the one, and the disadvantages arising from the other sort of men, we shall evidently see, that as the one is an excessive burden, curse, and reproach to us, so the other may enrich the nation, and adorn this country with public works beyond any in Europe, which shall not take the like methods of providing for their poor.

This proposal I hope may be a remedy, not only to that intolerable plague of idle vagabonds who infest the nation; but by providing a more regular maintenance for them, go a great way towards the present relief of other poor people who have been oppressed by them. That which follows is calculated to remove the principal and original cause of the poverty which all the commons of this nation lie under, as well as those straitening difficulties in which men of estates are by our present method of husbandry inevitably involved.

The causes of the present poverty and misery in which the commonalty of Scotland live, are many, yet they are all to be imputed to our own bad conduct and mismanagement of our affairs. It is true, trade being of late years vastly increased in Europe, the poverty of any nation is always imputed to their want of that advantage. And though our soil be barren, yet our seas being the richest of any in the world, it may be thought that the cause of all our poverty has been the neglect of trade, and chiefly of our own fishing: nevertheless were I to assign the principal and original source of our poverty, I should place it in the letting of our lands at so excessive a rate as makes the tenant poorer even than his servant whose wages he cannot pay; and involves in the same misery day-labourers, tradesmen, and the lesser merchants who live in the country villages and towns; and thereby influences no less the great towns and wholesale merchants, makes the master have a

58

troublesome and ill-paid rent, his lands not improved by enclosure or otherwise, but for want of horses and oxen fit for labour, everywhere run out and abused.

The condition of the lesser freeholders or heritors (as we call them) is not much better than that of our tenants; for they have no flocks to improve their lands, and living not as husbandmen but as gentlemen, they are never able to attain any: besides this, the unskilfulness of their wretched and half-starved servants is such, that their lands are no better cultivated than those laboured by beggarly tenants. And though a gentleman of estate take a farm into his own hands, yet servants are so unfaithful or lazy, and the country people such enemies of all manner of enclosure, that after having struggled with innumerable difficulties, he at last finds it impossible for him to alter the ordinary bad methods, whilst the rest of the country continues in them.

The places in this country which produce sheep and black cattle have no provision for them in winter during the snows, having neither hay nor straw, nor any enclosure to shelter them or the grass from the cold easterly winds in the spring; so that the beasts are in a dying condition, and the grass consumed by those destructive winds, till the warm weather, about the middle of June, come to the relief of both. To all this may be added the letting of farms in most part of those grazing countries every year by roop or auction. But our management in the countries cultivated by tillage is much worse, because the tenant pays his rent in grain, wheat, barley, or oats: which is attended with many inconveniences, and much greater disadvantages than a rent paid in money.

Money rent has a yearly balance in it; for if the year be scarce, all sorts of grain yield the greater price; and if the year be plentiful, there is the greater quantity of them to make money. Now a rent paid in corn has neither a yearly, nor any balance at all; for if a plentiful year afford a superplus, the tenant can make but little of it; but if the year be scarce, he falls short in the payment of his corn, and by reason of the price it bears, can never clear that debt by the rates of a plentiful year, by which means he breaks, and contributes to ruin his master. The rent being altogether in corn, the grounds must be altogether in tillage; which has been the ruin of all the best countries in Scotland. The carriage of corn paid for rent, to which many tenants are obliged, being often to remote places, and at unseasonable times, destroys their horses, and hinders their labour. And the hazard of sending the corn by sea to the great towns, endangers the loss of the whole. The master runs a double risk for his rent, from the merchant as well as the tenant; and the merchant making a thousand difficulties at the delivering of the corn if the price be fallen, the bargain sometimes ends in a suit at law. The selling of corn is become a thing so difficult, that besides the cheats used in that sort of commerce, sufficient to disgust any honest man, the brewers, bakers, and sometimes the merchants who send it abroad do so combine together, that the gentleman is obliged to lay it up, of which the trouble as well as loss is great. This causes him to borrow money for the supply of his present occasions, and is the beginning of most men's debts. We may add to this, that by a rent in corn, a man comes to have one year a thousand-pound rent, and the next perhaps but six hundred, so that he never can make any certain account for his expense or way of living; that having one year a thousand pound to spend, he cannot easily restrain himself to six hundred the next; that he spends the same quantity of corn (and in some places where such things are delivered instead of rent), hay, straw, poultry, sheep, and oxen in a dear, as in a plentiful year, which he would not do if he was obliged to buy them. Now the tenant in a plentiful year wastes, and in a scarce year starves: so that no man of any substance will take a farm in Scotland; but every beggar, if he have got half a dozen wretched horses, and as many oxen, and can borrow corn to sow, pretends to be a tenant in places where they pay no other rent than corn.

I know there are many objections made to what has been said concerning the advantages which a rent paid in money has above one paid in corn; but certainly they are all so frivolous, that every man upon a little reflection may answer them to himself. For the chief of them are, either that the tenant will squander away money when he gets it into his hands; or that the master can get a better price for the corn by selling it in gross to merchants in the adjacent towns, or else by sending it to be sold at a great distance. To the first I answer, that no substantial man will squander away money because he has got it into his hands, though such beggars as we now have for tenants might be apt to do so. And to the second, that the hazard of sending corn from one place of the kingdom to another by sea, and the prejudice the tenants suffer from long carriages by land, do in part balance the supposed advantage; besides, if those wholesale bargains were not so frequently made, nor the corn so often carried to be sold at the great towns, the merchants would be obliged to send to the country markets to buy, and the prices in them would rise. In short, the changing of money-rent into corn has been the chief cause of racking all the rents to that excessive rate they are now advanced. And upon reflection it will soon appear that the turning of money-rents into rents of corn has been the invention of some covetous wretches, who have been the occasion that all masters now live under the same uneasiness, and constant care, which they at first out of covetousness created to themselves; and all to get as much as was possible from poor tenants, who by such means are made miserable, and are so far from improving, that they only run out and spoil the ground, ruin their neighbours by borrowing, and at length break for considerable sums, though at first they were no better than beggars.

The method of most other countries is: that all rents are paid in money; that masters receiving a fine, grant long leases of their grounds at easy rents: but this supposes the tenant a man of considerable substance, who cannot only give a fine, but has wherewithal to stock, and also to improve his farm. But in Scotland no such men are willing to take farms; nor in truth are the masters willing to let them, as they do in other countries. And though the masters may pretend, that if they could find substantial tenants, they would let their grounds as they do in other places; and men of substance, that if they could have farms upon such conditions, they would turn tenants; yet we see evident marks of the little probability there is that any such thing can be brought about without a general regulation. For in the west and north countries where they let land in feu (or fee) the superiors are so hard, that besides the yearly feu-duty, they make the feuer pay at his first entrance the whole intrinsic value of the land; and the people, though substantial men, are fools and slaves enough to make such bargains. And in the same countries, when they let a small parcel of land to a tradesman, they let it not for what the land is worth, but what both the land and his trade is worth. And indeed it is next to an impossibility to alter a general bad custom in any nation, without a general regulation, because of inveterate bad dispositions and discouragements, with which the first beginnings of reformations are always attended. Besides, alterations that are not countenanced by the public authority proceed slowly; and if they chance to meet with any check, men soon return to their former bad methods.

The condition then of this nation, chiefly by this abuse of racking the lands, is brought to such extremity, as makes all the commonalty miserable, and the landlords, if possible, the greater slaves, before they can get their rents and reduce them into money. And because this evil is arrived to a greater height with us, than I believe was ever known in any other place; and that, as I have said, we are in no disposition to practise the methods of most other countries, I think we ought to find out some new one which may surmount all difficulties, since in things of this nature divers methods may be proposed very practicable, and much better than any that hitherto have been in use.

I know that if to a law prohibiting all interest for money, another were joined, that no man should possess more land than so much as he should cultivate by servants, the whole money, as well as people of this nation, would be presently employed, either in cultivating lands or in trade and manufactures; that the country would be quickly improved to the greatest height of which the soil is capable, since it would be cultivated by all the rich men of the nation; and that there would still be vast stocks remaining to be employed in trade and manufactures. But to oblige a man of a great estate in land to sell all, except perhaps two hundred pounds sterling a year (which he might cultivate by his servants) and to employ the whole money produced by the sale of the rest, in a thing so uncertain as he would judge trade to be, and for which it is like he might have no disposition or genius, being a thing impracticable: and also to employ the small stocks of minors, widows, and other women unmarried, in trade or husbandry, a thing of too great hazard for them; I would propose a method for our relief, by joining to the law prohibiting all interest of money, and to the other, that no man should possess more land than so much as he cultivates by his servants, a third law, obliging all men that possess lands under the value of two hundred pounds sterling clear profits yearly, to cultivate them by servants, and pay yearly the half of the clear profits to such persons as cultivating land worth two hundred pounds' sterling a year, or above, shall buy such rents of them at twenty years' purchase. The project in its full extent may be comprehended in these following articles.

All interest of money to be forbidden.

No man to possess more land than he cultivates by servants.

Every man cultivating land under the value of two hundred pounds' sterling clear profits a year, to pay yearly the half of the clear profits to some other man who shall buy that rent at twenty years' purchase; and for his security shall be preferred to all other creditors.

No man to buy or possess those rents, unless he cultivate land to the value at least of two hundred pounds' sterling clear profits yearly.

Minors, women unmarried, and persons absent upon a public account, may buy or possess such rents, though they cultivate no lands.

By the first article, discharging all interest of money, most men who have small sums at interest, will be obliged to employ it in trade, or the improvement of land.

By the second, that no man is to possess more land, than so much as he cultivates by his servants, the whole land of the kingdom will come into the hands of the richest men; at least there will be no land cultivated by any man who is not the possessor of it. And if he have a greater estate than what he cultivates, he may lay out money upon improvements; or if he have bought a small possession, though he may have no more money left, he may, by selling one half of the rent, procure a sum considerable enough, both to stock and improve it. So that in a few years the country will be everywhere enclosed and improved to the greatest height, the plough being everywhere in the hand of the possessor. Then servants, day-labourers, tradesmen, and all sorts of merchants will be well paid, and the whole commons live plentifully, because they will all be employed by men of substance: the ground by enclosure, and other improvements, will produce the double of what it now does; and the race of horses and black cattle will be much mended.

By the other articles: that no man cultivating land under the value of two hundred pounds' sterling clear profits yearly, can purchase rents upon land from any other man, but is obliged to pay yearly the half of the clear profits to such persons as shall buy them at twenty years' purchase; and that only those who cultivate land worth at least two hundred pounds' sterling a year can buy such rents; the men of great land estates having sold all their lands, except so much as may yield two hundred pounds' sterling yearly, or so much above that value as they shall think fit to cultivate, may secure, if they please, the whole money they receive for their lands, upon those rents which the lesser possessors are obliged to sell. And so those who had formerly their estates in lands ill cultivated, and corn-rents ill paid, as well as the other three sorts of persons excepted from the general rule, and mentioned in the last article, will have a clear rent in money coming in without trouble, for payment of which they are to be secured in the lands of the said lesser possessors before all creditors. The reason of excepting three sorts of persons before-mentioned from the general rule is evident; because (as has been said) it were unreasonable to oblige minors, or women unmarried, to venture their small stocks in trade or husbandry: and much more than those who are absent upon a public account, should be obliged to have any stock employed that way, since they cannot inspect either.

The small possessors by this project are not wronged in anything; for if they are obliged to pay a rent to others, they receive the value of it. And this rent will put them in mind, not to live after the manner of men of great estates, but as husbandmen, which will be no way derogatory to their quality, however ancient their family may be.

The method to put this project in execution is, first to enact; that interest for money should fall next year from six per cent. to five, and so on, falling every year one per cent. till it cease: and to make a law, that all those who at present possess lands under the value of two hundred pounds' sterling clear profits yearly, should cultivate them by servants, and sell the half of the clear profits at twenty years' purchase to the first minor, woman unmarried, or person absent upon a public account who should offer money for them; and in default of such persons presenting themselves to buy, they should be obliged to sell such rents to any other persons qualified as above: and likewise to make another law, that whoever possesses lands at present to the value of two hundred pounds' sterling clear profits yearly, or more, should at least take so much of them as may amount to that value, into their own hands. This being done, the yearly falling of the interest of money would force some of those who might have money at interest, to take land for it: others calling for their money would buy estates of the landed men, who are to sell all except so much as they cultivate themselves: and the prohibition of interest producing many small possessors would afford abundance of rents upon land to be bought by rich men; of which many might probably be paid out of those very lands they themselves formerly possessed. So that all sorts of men would in a little time fall into that easy method for their affairs, which is proposed by the project.

What the half of the yearly clear profits of any small possessors may be, the usual valuation of lands, in order to public taxes, which because of improvements must be frequently made, will ascertain.

But it will be said, that before any such thing can everywhere take place in this nation, all teinds (or tithes) and all sorts of superiorities, must be transacted for, and sold; that the tenures of all lands must be made allodial, to the end that every man may be upon an equal foot with another; that this project, in order to its execution, does suppose things, which though perhaps they would be great blessings to the nation upon many accounts, and in particular by taking away the seeds of most law-suits, and the obstructions to all sorts of improvements; yet are in themselves as great and considerable as the project itself.

Indeed I must acknowledge that anything calculated for a good end is (since we must express it so) almost always clogged with things of the same nature: for as all bad, so all good things are chained together, and do support one another. But that there is any difficulty, to a legislative power (that is willing to do good) of putting either this project, or the things last named in execution, I believe no man can show. Sure I am, that it never was nor can be the interest of any prince or commonwealth, that any subject should in any manner depend upon another subject: and that it is the interest of all good governments at least to encourage a good sort of husbandry.

I know these proposals, by some men who aim at nothing but private interest, will be looked upon as visionary: it is enough for me, that in themselves, and with regard to the nature of the things, they are practicable; but if on account of the indisposition of such men to receive them, they be thought impracticable, it is not to be accounted strange; since if that indisposition ought only to be considered, everything directed to a good end is such.

Many other proposals might be made to the parliament for the good of this nation, where everything is so much amiss, and the public good so little regarded. Amongst other things, to remove the present seat of the government, might deserve their consideration: for as the happy situation of London has been the principal cause of the glory and riches of England, so the bad situation of Edinburgh has been one great occasion of the poverty and uncleanliness in which the greater part of the people of Scotland live.

A proposal likewise for the better education of our youth would be very necessary: and I must confess I know no part of the world where education is upon any tolerable foot. But perhaps I have presumed too much in offering my opinion upon such considerable matters as those which I have treated.

Since I finished the preceding discourses I am informed, that if the present parliament will not comply with the design of continuing the army, they shall immediately be dissolved, and a new one called. At least those of the presbyterian persuasion, who expect no good from a new parliament, are to be frightened with the dissolution of the present (which has established their church-government) and by that means induced to use their utmost endeavours with the members for keeping up the army, and promoting the designs of ill men: but I hope no presbyterian will ever be for evil things that good may come of them; since thereby they may draw a curse upon themselves instead of a blessing. They will certainly consider that the interest which they ought to embrace, as well upon the account of prudence, as of justice and duty, is that of their country; and will not hearken to the insinuations of ill men who may abuse them, and when they have obtained the continuation of the army, endeavour to persuade his majesty and the parliament, to alter the present government of the church, by telling them that presbyterian government is in its nature opposite to monarchy, that they maintain a rebellious principle of defensive arms, and that a church-government more suitable and subservient to monarchy ought to be established.

Now if at this time the presbyterians be true to the interest of their country, all those who love their country, though they be not of that persuasion, will stand by them in future parliaments, when they shall see that they oppose all things tending to arbitrary power: but if they abandon and betray their country, they will fall unpitied. They must not tell me that their church can never fall, since it is the true church of God. If it be the true church of God, it needs no crooked arts to support it. But I hope they will not deny that it may fall under persecution; which they will deserve, if they go along with the least ill thing to maintain it.

SPEECHES

BY A

Member of the PARLIAMENT

WHICH

Began at Edinburgh the 6th of May, 1703.

Edinburgh;

Printed in the Year MDCCIII.

ADVERTISEMENT

Some of the following Speeches are not placed in the order they were spoken, but in such an order as the matters they contain seem to require.

I

My Lord Chancellor

I am not surprised to find an act for a supply brought into this house at the beginning of a session. I know custom has for a long time made it common. But I think experience might teach us that such acts should be the last of every session; or lie upon the table, until all other great affairs of the nation be finished, and then only granted. It is a strange proposition which is usually made in this house, that if we will give money to the crown, then the crown will give us good laws: as if we were to buy good laws of the crown, and pay money to our princes, that they may do their duty, and comply with their coronation oath. And yet this is not the worst; for we have often had promises of good laws, and when we have given the sums demanded, those promises have been broken, and the nation left to seek a remedy; which is not to be found, unless we obtain the laws we want, before we give a supply. And if this be a sufficient reason at all times to postpone a money-act, can we be blamed for doing so at this time, when the duty we owe to our country indispensably obliges us to provide for the common safety in case of an event, altogether out of our power, and which must necessarily dissolve the government, unless we continue and secure it by new laws; I mean the death of her Majesty, which God in his mercy long avert? I move, therefore, that the house would take into consideration what acts are necessary to secure our religion, liberty, and trade, in case of the said event, before any act of supply, or other business whatever be brought into deliberation.

Act concerning offices, &c. brought in by the same member

The estates of Parliament taking into their consideration, that to the great loss and detriment of this nation, great sums of money are yearly carried out of it, by those who wait and depend at court, for places and preferments in this kingdom: and that by Scotsmen, employing English interest at court, in order to obtain their several pretensions, this nation is in hazard of being brought to depend upon English ministers: and likewise considering, that by reason our princes do no more reside amongst us, they cannot be rightly informed of the merit of persons pretending to places, offices, and pensions; therefore our Sovereign Lady, with advice and consent of the estates of parliament, statutes and ordains, that after the decease of her Majesty (whom God long preserve) and heirs of her body failing, all places and offices, both civil and military, and all pensions, formerly conferred by our Kings, shall ever after be given by parliament, by way of ballot.

II

My Lord Chancellor

When our Kings succeeded to the crown of England, the ministers of that nation took a short way to ruin us, by concurring with their inclinations to extend the prerogative in Scotland; and the great places and pensions conferred upon Scotsmen by that court, made them to be willing instruments in the work. From that time this nation began to give away their privileges one after the other, though they then stood more in need of having them enlarged. And as the collections of our laws, before the union of the crowns, are full of acts to secure our liberty, those laws that have been made since that time are directed chiefly to extend the prerogative. And that we might not know what rights and liberties were still ours, nor be excited by the memory of what our ancestors enjoyed, to recover those we had lost, in the two last editions of our acts of parliament the most considerable laws for the liberty of the subject are industriously and designedly left out. All our affairs since the union of the crowns have been managed by the advice of English ministers, and the principal offices of the kingdom filled with such men, as the court of England knew would be subservient to their designs: by which means they have had so visible an influence upon our whole administration, that we have from that time appeared to the rest of the world more like a conquered province than a free independent people. The account is very short: whilst our princes are not absolute in England, they must be influenced by that nation; our ministers must follow the directions of the prince, or lose their places, and our places and pensions will be distributed according to the inclinations of a king of England, so long as a king of England has the disposal of them: neither shall any man obtain the least advancement, who refuses to vote in council and parliament under that influence. So that there is no way to free this country from a ruinous dependence upon the English court, unless by placing the power of conferring offices and pensions in the parliament, so long as we shall have the same king with England. The ancient Kings of Scotland, and even those of France, had not the power of conferring the chief offices of state, though each of them had only one kingdom to govern, and that the difficulty we labour under, of two kingdoms which have different interests governed by the same king, did not occur. Besides, we all know that the disposal of our places and pensions is so considerable a thing to a king of England, that several of our princes, since the union of the crowns, have wished to be free from the trouble of deciding between the many pretenders. That which would have given them ease, will give us liberty, and make us significant to the common interest of both nations. Without this, it is impossible to free us from a dependence on the English court: all other remedies and conditions of government will prove ineffectual, as plainly appears from the nature of the thing; for who is not sensible of the influence of places and pensions upon all men and all affairs? If our ministers continue to be appointed by the English court, and this nation may not be permitted to dispose of the offices and places of this kingdom to balance the English bribery, they will corrupt everything to that degree, that if any of our laws stand in their way, they will get them repealed. Let no man say, that it cannot be proved that the English court has ever bestowed any bribe in this country. For they bestow all offices and pensions; they bribe us, and are masters of us at our own cost. It is nothing but an English interest in this house, that those who wish well to our country, have to struggle with at this time. We may, if we please, dream of other remedies; but so long as Scotsmen must go to the English court to obtain offices of trust or profit in this kingdom, those offices will always be managed with regard to the court and interest of England, though to the betraying of the interest of this nation, whenever it comes in competition with that of England. And what less can be expected, unless we resolve to expect miracles, and that greedy, ambitious, and for the most part necessitous men, involved in great debts, burdened with great families, and having great titles to support, will lay down their places, rather than comply with an English interest in obedience to the prince's commands? Now to find Scotsmen opposing this, and willing that English ministers (for this is the case) should have the disposal of places and pensions in Scotland, rather than their own parliament, is matter of great astonishment; but that it should be so much as a question in the parliament, is altogether incomprehensible: and if an indifferent person were to judge, he would certainly say we were an English parliament. Every man knows that princes give places and pensions by the influence of those who advise them. So that the question comes to no more than, whether this nation would be in a better condition, if in conferring our places and pensions the prince should be determined by the parliament of Scotland, or by the ministers of a court, that make it their interest to keep us low and miserable. We all know that this is the cause of our poverty, misery, and dependence. But we have been for a long time so poor, so miserable and depending, that we have neither heart nor courage, though we want not the means, to free ourselves.

III

My Lord Chancellor

Prejudice and opinion govern the world to the great distress and ruin of mankind; and though we daily find men so rational as to charm by the disinterested rectitude of their sentiments in all other things, yet when we touch upon any wrong opinion with which they have been early prepossessed, we find them more irrational than anything in nature; and not only not to be convinced, but obstinately resolved not to hear any reason against it. These prejudices are yet stronger when they are taken up by great numbers of men, who confirm each other through the course of several generations, and seem to have their blood tainted, or, to speak more properly, their animal spirits influenced by them. Of these delusions, one of the strongest and most pernicious has been a violent inclination in many men to extend the prerogative of the prince to an absolute and unlimited power. And though in limited monarchies all good men profess and declare themselves enemies to all tyrannical practices, yet many, even of these, are found ready to oppose such necessary limitations as might secure them from the tyrannical exercise of power in a prince, not only subject to all the infirmities of other men, but by the temptations arising from his power, to far greater. This humour has greatly increased in our nation since the union of the crowns; and the slavish submissions, which have been made necessary to procure the favours of the court, have cherished and fomented a slavish principle. But I must take leave to put the representatives of this nation in mind, that no such principles were in this kingdom before the union of the crowns; and that no monarchy in Europe was more limited, nor any people more jealous of liberty than the Scots. These principles were first introduced among us after the union of the crowns, and the prerogative extended to the overthrow of our ancient constitution, chiefly by the prelatical party; though the peevish, imprudent, and detestable conduct of the presbyterians, who opposed these principles only in others, drove many into them, gave them greater force, and rooted them more deeply in this nation. Should we not be ashamed to embrace opinions contrary to reason, and contrary to the sentiments of our ancestors, merely upon account of the uncharitable and insupportable humour and ridiculous conduct of bigots of any sort? If then no such principles were in this nation, and the constitution of our government had greatly limited the prince's power before the union of the crowns; dare any man say he is a Scotsman, and refuse his consent to reduce the government of this nation, after the expiration of the entail, within the same limits as before that union? And if since the union of the crowns everyone sees that we stand in need of more limitations, will any man act in so direct an opposition to his own reason, and the undoubted interest of his country, as not to concur in limiting the government yet more than before the union, particularly by the addition of this so necessary limitation for which I am now speaking? My Lord, these are such clear demonstrations of what we ought to do in such conjunctures, that all men of common ingenuity must be ashamed of entering into any other measures. Let us not then tread in the steps of mean and fawning priests of any sort, who are always disposed to place an absolute power in the prince, if he on his part will gratify their ambition, and by all means support their form of church-government, to the persecution of all other men who will not comply with their impositions. Let us begin where our ancestors left before the union of the crowns, and be for the future more jealous of our liberties, because there is more need. But I must take upon me to say, that he who is not for setting great limitations upon the power of the prince, particularly that for which I am speaking, in case we have the same king with England, can act by no principle, whether he be a presbyterian, prelatical, or prerogative-man, for the court of St. Germains, or that of Hanover; I say, he can act by no principle unless that of being a slave to the court of England for his own advantage. And therefore let not those who go under the name of prerogative-men cover themselves with the pretext of principles in this case; for such men are plainly for the prerogative of the English court over this nation, because this limitation is demanded only in case we come to have the same king with England.

Act for the security of the kingdom, brought in by the same member

The estates of parliament considering, that when it shall please God to afflict this nation with the death of our Sovereign Lady the Queen (whom God of his infinite mercy long preserve) if the same shall happen to be without heirs of her body, this kingdom may fall into great confusion and disorder before a successor can be declared. For preventing thereof, our Sovereign Lady, with advice and consent of the estates of parliament, statutes and ordains, that if at the foresaid time, any parliament or convention of estates shall be assembled, then the members of that parliament or convention of estates shall take the administration of the government upon them: excepting those barons and burghs, who at the foresaid time shall have any place or pension, mediately or immediately of the crown: whose commissions are hereby declared to be void; and that new members shall be chosen in their place: but if there be no parliament or convention of estates actually assembled, then the members of the current parliament shall assemble with all possible diligence: and if there be no current parliament, then the members of the last dissolved parliament, or convention of estates, shall assemble in like manner: and in those two last cases, so soon as there shall be one hundred members met, in which number the barons and burghs before-mentioned are not to be reckoned, they shall take the administration of the government upon them: but neither they, nor the members of parliament, or convention of estates, if at the time foresaid assembled, shall proceed to the weighty affair of naming and declaring a successor, until twenty days after they have assumed the administration of the government: both that there may be time for all the other members to come to Edinburgh, which is hereby declared the place of their meeting, and for the elections of new barons and burghs in place above-mentioned. But so soon as the twenty days are elapsed, then they shall proceed to the publishing by proclamation the conditions of government, on which they will receive the successor to the imperial crown of this realm; which in the case only of our being under the same king with England, are as follows.

1. That elections shall be made at every Michaelmas head-court for a new parliament every year; to sit the first of November next following, and adjourn themselves from time to time, till next Michaelmas: that they choose

their own president, and that everything shall be determined by balloting, in place of voting.

2. That so many lesser barons shall be added to the parliament, as there have been noblemen created since the last augmentation of the number of the barons; and that in all time coming, for every nobleman that shall be created, there shall be a baron added to the parliament.

3. That no man have vote in parliament, but a nobleman or elected member.

4. That the king shall give the sanction to all laws offered by the estates; and that the president of the parliament be empowered by his majesty to give the sanction in his absence, and have ten pounds sterling a day salary.

5. That a committee of one and thirty members, of which nine to be a quorum, chosen out of their number, by every parliament, shall, during the intervals of parliament, under the king, have the administration of the government, be his council, and accountable to the next parliament; with power in extraordinary occasions, to call the parliament together: and that in the said council, all things be determined by balloting in place of voting.

6. That the king without consent of parliament shall not have the power of making peace and war; or that of concluding any treaty with any other state or potentate.

7. That all places and offices, both civil and military, and all pensions formerly conferred by our kings, shall ever after be given by parliament.

8. That no regiment or company of horse, foot, or dragoons be kept on foot in peace or war, but by consent of parliament.

9. That all the fencible men of the nation, betwixt sixty and fifteen, be with all diligence possible armed with bayonets, and firelocks all of a calibre, and continue always provided in such arms with ammunition suitable.

10. That no general indemnity, nor pardon for any transgression against the public, shall be valid without consent of parliament.

11. That the fifteen senators of the college of justice shall be incapable of being members of parliament, or of any other office, or any pension: but the salary that belongs to their place to be increased as the parliament shall think fit: that the office of president shall be in three of their number to be named by parliament, and that there be no extraordinary lords. And also, that the lords of the justice court shall be distinct from those of the session, and under the same restrictions.

12. That if any king break in upon any of these conditions of government, he shall by the estates be declared to have forfeited the crown.

Which proclamation made, they are to go on to the naming and declaring a successor: and when it is declared, if present, are to read to him the claim of right and conditions of government above-mentioned, and to desire of him, that he may accept the crown accordingly; and he accepting, they are to administer to him the oath of coronation: but if the successor be not present, they are to delegate such of their own number as they shall think fit, to see the same performed, as said is: and are to continue in the administration of the government, until the successor his accepting of the crown, upon the foresaid terms be known to them: whereupon having then a king at their head, they shall by his authority declare themselves a parliament, and proceed to the doing of whatever shall be thought expedient for the welfare of the realm. And it is likewise by the authority aforesaid declared, that if her present majesty shall think fit, during her own time, with advice and consent of the estates of parliament, failing heirs of her body, to declare a successor, yet nevertheless, after her Majesty's decease, the members of parliament or convention shall in the several cases, and after the manner above-specified, meet and admit the successor to the government, in the terms and after the manner as said is. And it is hereby further declared, that after the decease of her Majesty, and failing heirs of her body, the fore-mentioned manner and method shall in the several cases be that of declaring and admitting to the government all those who shall hereafter succeed to the imperial crown of this realm; and that it shall be high treason for any man to own or acknowledge any person as king or queen of this realm, till they are declared and admitted in the above-mentioned manner. And lastly, it is hereby declared, that by the death of her Majesty, or any of her successors, all commissions, both civil and military, fall and are void. And that this act shall come in place of the seventeenth act of the sixth session of King William's parliament. And all acts and laws, that anyway derogate from this present act, are hereby in so far declared void and abrogated.

IV

My Lord Chancellor

It is the utmost height of human prudence to see and embrace every favourable opportunity: and if a word spoken in season does for the most part produce wonderful effects; of what consequence and advantage must it be to a nation in deliberations of the highest moment; in occasions, when passed, for ever irretrievable, to enter into the right path, and take hold of the golden opportunity, which makes the most arduous things easy, and without which the most inconsiderable may put a stop to all our affairs? We have this day an opportunity in our hands which if we manage to the advantage of the nation we have the honour to represent, we may, so far as the vicissitude and uncertainty of human affairs will permit, be for many ages easy and happy. But if we despise or neglect this occasion, we have voted our perpetual dependence on another nation. If men could always retain those just impressions of things they at sometimes have upon their minds, they would be much more steady in their actions. And as I may boldly say, that no man is to be found in this house, who at some time or other has not had that just sense of the miserable condition to which this nation is reduced by a dependence upon the English court, I should demand no more but the like impressions at this time to pass all the limitations mentioned in the draught of an act I have already brought into this house; since they are not limitations upon any prince, who shall only be king of Scotland, nor do any way tend to separate us from England; but calculated merely to this end, that so long as we continue to be under the same prince with our neighbour nation, we may be free from the influence of English councils and ministers; that the nation may not be impoverished by an expensive attendance at court, and that the force and exercise of our government may be, as far as is possible, within ourselves. By which means trade, manufactures, and husbandry will flourish, and the affairs of the nation be no longer neglected, as they have been hitherto. These are the ends to which all the limitations are directed, that English councils may not hinder the acts of our parliaments from receiving the royal assent; that we may not be engaged without our consent in the quarrels they may have with other nations; that they may not obstruct the meeting of our parliaments, nor interrupt their sitting; that we may not stand in need of posting to London for places and pensions, by which, whatever particular men may get, the nation must always be a loser, nor apply for the remedies of our grievances to a court, where for the most part none are to be had. On the contrary, if these conditions of government be enacted, our constitution will be amended, and our grievances be easily redressed by a due execution of our own laws, which to this day we have never been able to obtain. The best and wisest men in England will be glad to hear that these limitations are settled by us. For though the ambition of courtiers lead them to desire an uncontrollable power at any rate; yet wiser men will consider that when two nations live under the same prince, the condition of the one cannot be made intolerable, but a separation must inevitably follow, which will be dangerous if not destructive to both. The senate of Rome wisely determined in the business of the Privernates, that all people would take hold of the first opportunity to free themselves from an uneasy condition; that no peace could be lasting, in which both parties did not find their account; and that no alliance was strong enough to keep two nations in amity, if the condition of either were made worse by it. For my own part, my lord Chancellor, before I will consent to continue in our present miserable and languishing condition after the decease of her Majesty, and heirs of her body failing, I shall rather give my vote for a separation from England at any rate. I hope no man who is now possessed of an office will take umbrage at these conditions of government, though some of them seem to diminish, and others do entirely suppress the place he possesses: for besides the scandal of preferring a private interest before that of our country, these limitations are not to take place immediately. The Queen is yet young, and by the grace of God may live many years, I hope longer than all those she has placed in any trust; and should we not be happy, if those who for the future may design to recommend themselves for any office, could not do it by any other way than the favour of this house, which they who appear for these conditions will deserve in a more eminent degree? Would we rather court an English minister for a place than a parliament of Scotland? Are we afraid of being taken out of the hands of English courtiers, and left to govern ourselves? And do we doubt whether an English ministry, or a Scots parliament will be most for the interest of Scotland? But that which seems most difficult in this question, and in which, if satisfaction be given, I hope no man will pretend to be dissatisfied with these limitations, is the interest of a king of Great Britain. And here I shall take liberty to say, that as the limitations do no way affect any prince that may be king of Scotland only, so they will be found highly advantageous to a king of Great Britain. Some of our late kings, when they have been perplexed about the affairs of Scotland, did let fall such expressions, as intimated they thought them not worth their application. And indeed we ought not to wonder if princes, like other men, should grow weary of toiling where they find no advantage. But to set this affair in a true light: I desire to know, whether it can be more advantageous to a king of Great Britain to have an unlimited prerogative over this country in our present ill condition, which turns to no account, than that this nation grown rich and powerful under these conditions of government, should be able upon any emergency to furnish a good body of land forces, with a squadron of ships for war, all paid by ourselves, to assist his Majesty in the wars he may undertake for the defence of the protestant religion and liberties of Europe. Now since I hope I have shown that those who are for the prerogative of the kings of Scotland, and all those who are possessed of places at this time, together with the whole English nation, as well as a king of Great Britain, have cause to be satisfied with these regulations of government, I would know what difficulty can remain; unless that being accustomed to live in a dependency and unacquainted with liberty, we know not so much as the meaning of the word; nor if that should be explained to us, can ever persuade ourselves we shall obtain the thing, though we have it in our power by a few votes to set ourselves and our posterity free. To say that this will stop at the royal assent, is a suggestion disrespectful to her Majesty, and which ought neither to be mentioned in parliament, nor be considered by any member of this house. And were this a proper time, I am confident I could say such things as being represented to the Queen would convince her, that no person can have greater interest, nor obtain more lasting honour by the enacting of these conditions of government, than her Majesty. And if the nation be assisted in this exigency by the good offices of his grace the high Commissioner, I shall not doubt to affirm, that in procuring this blessing to our country from her Majesty, he will do more for us than all the great men of that noble family, of which he is descended, ever did; though it seems to have been their peculiar province for divers ages to defend the liberties of this nation against the power of the English and the deceit of courtiers. What further arguments can I use to persuade this house to enact these limitations, and embrace this occasion, which we have so little deserved? I might bring many; but the most proper and effectual to persuade all, I take to be this: that our ancestors did enjoy the most essential liberties contained in the act I have proposed: and though some few of less moment are among them which they had not, yet they were in possession of divers others not contained in these articles: that they enjoyed these privileges when they were separated from England, had their prince living among them, and consequently stood not in so great need of these limitations. Now since we have been under the same prince with England, and therefore stand in the greatest need of them, we have not only neglected to make a due provision of that kind, but in divers parliaments have given away our liberties, and upon the matter subjected this crown to the court of England: and are become so accustomed to depend on them, that we seem to doubt whether we shall lay hold of this happy opportunity to resume our freedom. If nothing else will move us, at least let us not act in opposition to the light of our own reason and conscience, which daily represents to us the ill constitution of our government; the low condition into which we are sunk, and the extreme poverty, distress, and misery of our people. Let us consider whether we will have the nation continue in these deplorable circumstances, and lose this opportunity of bringing freedom and plenty among us. Sure the heart of every honest man must bleed daily, to see the misery in which our commons, and even many of our gentry live; which has no other cause but the ill constitution of our government, and our bad government no other root, but our dependence upon the court of England. If our kings lived among us, it would not be strange to find these limitations rejected. It is not the prerogative of a king of Scotland I would diminish, but the prerogative of English ministers over this nation. To conclude, these conditions of government being either such as our ancestors enjoyed, or principally directed to cut off our dependence on an English court, and not to take place during the life of the Queen; he who refuses his consent to them, whatever he may be by birth, cannot sure be a Scotsman by affection. This will be a true test to distinguish, not whig from tory, presbyterian from episcopal, Hanover from St. Germains, nor yet a courtier from a man out of place, but a proper test to distinguish a friend from an enemy to his country. And indeed we are split into so many parties, and cover ourselves with so many false pretexts, that such a test seems necessary to bring us into the light, and show every man in his own colours. In a word, my lord Chancellor, we are to consider, that though we suffer under many grievances, yet our dependence upon the court of England is the cause of all, comprehends them all, and is the band that ties up the bundle. If we break this, they will all drop and fall to the ground: if not, this band will straiten us more and more, till we shall be no longer a people.

I therefore humbly propose, that for the security of our religion, liberty, and trade, these limitations be declared by a resolution of this house to be the conditions upon which the nation will receive a successor to the crown of this realm after the decease of her present Majesty, and failing heirs of her body, in case the said successor shall be also King or Queen of England.

V

My Lord Chancellor

I am sorry to hear what has been just now spoken from the throne. I know the duty I owe to her Majesty, and the respect that is due to her

Commissioner; and therefore shall speak with a just regard to both. But the duty I owe to my country obliges me to say, that what we have now heard from the throne, must of necessity proceed from English councils. If we had demanded that these limitations should take place during the life of her Majesty, or of the heirs of her body, perhaps we might have no great reason to complain, though they should be refused. But that her Majesty should prefer the prerogative of she knows not who, to the happiness of the whole people of Scotland; that she should deny her assent to such conditions of government as are not limitations upon the crown of Scotland, but only such as are absolutely necessary to relieve us from a subjection to the court of England, must proceed from English councils; as well because there is no Scots minister now at London, as because I have had an account, which I believe to be too well grounded, that a letter to this effect has been sent down hither by the lord Treasurer of England, not many days ago. Besides, all men who have lately been at London, well know, that nothing has been more common, than to see Scotsmen of the several parties addressing themselves to English ministers about Scots affairs; and even to some ladies of that court, whom for the respect I bear to their relations I shall not name. Now, whether we shall continue under the influence and subjection of the English court; or whether it be not high time to lay before her Majesty, by a vote of this house, the conditions of government upon which we will receive a successor, I leave to the wisdom of the parliament. This I must say, that to tell us anything of her Majesty's intentions in this affair, before we have presented any act to that purpose for the royal assent, is to prejudge the cause, and altogether unparliamentary. I will add, that nothing has ever shown the power and force of English councils upon our affairs in a more eminent manner at any time, since the union of the crowns. No man in this house is more convinced of the great advantage of that peace which both nations enjoy by living under one prince. But as on the one hand, some men for private ends, and in order to get into offices, have either neglected or betrayed the interest of this nation, by a mean compliance with the English court; so on the other side it cannot be denied, that we have been but indifferently used by the English nation. I shall not insist upon the affair of Darien, in which by their means and influence chiefly, we suffered so great a loss both in men and money, as to put us almost beyond hope of ever having any considerable trade; and this contrary to their own true interest, which now appears but too visibly. I shall not go about to enumerate instances

81

of a provoking nature in other matters, but keep myself precisely to the thing we are upon. The English nation did, some time past, take into consideration the nomination of a successor to that crown; an affair of the highest importance, and one would think of common concernment to both kingdoms. Did they ever require our concurrence? Did they ever desire the late King to cause the parliament of Scotland to meet, in order to take our advice and consent? Was not this to tell us plainly, that we ought to be concluded by their determinations, and were not worthy to be consulted in the matter? Indeed, my lord Chancellor, considering their whole carriage in this affair, and the broad insinuations we have now heard, that we are not to expect her Majesty's assent to any limitations on a successor (which must proceed from English council) and considering we cannot propose to ourselves any other relief from that servitude we lie under by the influence of that court; it is my opinion that the house come to a resolution, *that after the decease of her Majesty, heirs of her body failing, we will separate our crown from that of England.*

VI

My Lord Chancellor

That there should be limitations on a successor, in order to take away our dependence on the court of England, if both nations should have the same king, no man here seems to oppose. And I think very few will be of opinion that such limitations should be deferred till the meeting of the nation's representatives upon the decease of her Majesty. For if the successor be not named before that time, everyone will be so earnest to promote the pretensions of the person he most affects, that new conditions will be altogether forgotten. So that those who are only in appearance for these limitations, and in reality against them, endeavour for their last refuge to mislead well-meaning men, by telling them, that it is not advisable to put them into the act of security, as well for fear of losing all, as because they will be more conveniently placed in a separate act. My lord Chancellor, I would fain know if anything can be more proper in an act which appoints the naming and manner of admitting a successor, than the conditions on which we agree to receive him. I would know, if the deferring of anything, at a time when naturally it should take place, be not to put a slur upon it, and an endeavour to defeat it. And if the limitations in question are pre-

82

tended to be such a burden in the act, as to hazard the loss of the whole, can we expect to obtain them when separated from the act? Is there any common sense in this? Let us not deceive ourselves, and imagine that the act of 1696 does not expire immediately after the Queen and heirs of her body; for in all that act, the heirs and successors of his late Majesty King William are always restrained and specified by these express words, 'according to the declaration of the estates, dated the 11th of April 1689.' So that unless we make a due provision by some new law, a dissolution of the government will ensue immediately upon the death of her Majesty, failing heirs of her body. Such an act therefore being of absolute and indispensable necessity, I am of opinion, that the limitations ought to be inserted therein as the only proper place for them, and surest way to obtain them: and that whoever would separate them, does not so much desire we should obtain the act, as that we should lose the limitations.

VII

My Lord Chancellor

I hope I need not inform this honourable house, that all acts which can be proposed for the security of this kingdom, are vain and empty propositions, unless they are supported by arms; and that to rely upon any law without such a security is to lean upon a shadow. We had better never pass this act: for then we shall not imagine we have done anything for our security; and if we think we can do anything effectual without that provision, we deceive ourselves, and are in a most danger-ous condition. Such an act cannot be said to be an act for the security of anything, in which the most necessary clause is wanting, and without which all the rest is of no force: neither can any kingdom be really secured but by arming the people. Let no man pretend that we have standing forces to support this law; and that if their numbers be not sufficient, we may raise more. It is very well known this nation cannot maintain so many standing forces as would be necessary for our defence, though we could entirely rely upon their fidelity. The pos-session of arms is the distinction of a freeman from a slave. He who has nothing, and belongs to another, must be defended by him, and needs no arms: but he who thinks he is his own master, and has any-thing he may call his own, ought to have arms to defend himself and what he possesses, or else he lives precariously and at discretion. And though for a while those who have the sword in their power abstain from doing him injuries; yet by degrees he will be awed into a submission to every arbitrary command. Our ancestors by being always armed, and frequently in action, defended themselves against the Romans, Danes, and English; and maintained their liberty against the encroachments of their own princes. If we are not rich enough to pay a sufficient number of standing forces, we have at least this advantage, that arms in our own hands serve no less to maintain our liberty at home than to defend us from enemies abroad. Other nations, if they think they can trust standing forces, may by their means defend themselves against foreign enemies. But we, who have not wealth sufficient to pay such forces, should not, of all nations under heaven, be unarmed. For us then to continue without arms, is to be directly in the condition of slaves: to be found unarmed in the event of her Majesty's death, would be to have no manner of security for our liberty, property, or the independence of this kingdom. By being unarmed, we every day run the risk of our all, since we know not how soon that event may overtake us: to continue still unarmed, when by this very act now under deliberation, we have put a case, which happening may spearate us from England, would be the grossest of all follies. And if we do not provide for arming the kingdom in such an exigency, we shall become a jest and a proverb to the world.

VIII

My Lord Chancellor

If in the sad event of her Majesty's decease without heirs of her body, any considerable military force should be in the hands of one or more men, who might have an understanding together, we are not very sure what use they would make of them in so nice and critical a conjuncture. We know that as the most just and honourable enterprises, when they fail, are accounted in the number of rebellions; so all attempts, however unjust, if they succeed, always purge themselves of all guilt and imputation. If a man presume he shall have success, and obtain the utmost of his hopes, he will not too nicely examine the point of right, nor balance too scrupulously the injury he does to his country. I would not have any man take this for a reflection upon those honourable persons, who have at present the command of our troops. For besides that we are not certain who shall be in those commands at the time of such an event, we are to know that all men are frail, and the wicked and mean-spirited world has paid too much honour to many, who have subverted the liberties of their country. We see a great disposition at this time in some men, not to consent to any limitations on a successor, though we should name the same with England. And therefore since this is probably the last opportunity we shall ever have of freeing ourselves from our dependence on the English court, we ought to manage it with the utmost jealousy and diffidence of such men. For though we have ordered the nation to be armed and exercised, which will be a sufficient defence when done: yet we know not but the event, which God avert, may happen before this can be effected. And we may easily imagine, what a few bold men, at the head of a small number of regular troops, might do, when all things are in confusion and suspense. So that we ought to make effectual provision with the utmost circumspection, that all such forces may be subservient to the government and interest of this nation, and not to the private ambition of their commanders. I therefore move, that immediately upon the decease of her Majesty, all military commissions above that of a captain be null and void.

IX

My Lord Chancellor

I know it is the undoubted prerogative of her Majesty, that no act of this house shall have the force of a law without her royal assent. And as I am confident his grace the high Commissioner is sufficiently instructed, to give that assent to every act which shall be laid before him; so more particularly to the act for the security of the kingdom, which has already passed this house: an act that preserves us from anarchy: an act that arms a defenceless people: an act that has cost the representatives of this kingdom much time and labour to frame, and the nation a very great expense: an act that has passed by a great majority: and above all an act that contains a caution of the highest importance for the amendment of our constitution. I did not presume the other day, immediately after this act was voted, to desire the royal assent; I thought it a just deference to the high Commissioner, not to mention it at that time. Neither would I now, but only that I may have an opportunity to represent to his grace, that as he who gives readily doubles the gift; so his grace has now in his hands the most glorious and honourable occasion that any person of this nation ever had, of making himself acceptable, and his memory for ever grateful to the people of this kingdom: since the honour of giving the royal assent to a law, which lays a lasting foundation for their liberties, has been reserved to him.

X

My Lord Chancellor

On the day that the act for the security of the kingdom passed in this house, I did not presume to move for the royal assent. The next day of our meeting I mentioned it with all imaginable respect and deference for his grace the high Commissioner, and divers honourable persons seconded me. If now, after the noble lord who spoke last, I insist upon it, I think I am no way to be blamed. I shall not endeavour to show the necessity of this act, in which the whole security of the nation now lies, having spoken to that point the other day: but shall take occasion to say something concerning the delay of giving the royal assent to acts passed in this house; for which I could never hear a good reason, except that a Commissioner was not sufficiently instructed. But that cannot be the true reason at this time, because several acts have lain long for the royal assent: in particular, that to ratify a former act, for turning the convention into a parliament, and fencing the claim of right, which no man doubts his grace is sufficiently instructed to pass. We must therefore look elsewhere for the reason of this delay, and ought to be excused in doing this; since so little regard is had, and so little satisfaction given to the representatives of this nation, who have for more than three months employed themselves with the greatest assiduity in the service of their country, and yet have not seen the least fruit of their labours crowned with the royal assent. Only one act has been touched, for recognizing her Majesty's just right, which is a thing of course. This gives but too good reason to those who speak freely, to say that the royal assent is industriously suspended, in order to oblige some men to vote, as shall be most expedient to a certain interest; and that this session of parliament is continued so long, chiefly to make men uneasy, who have neither places nor pensions to bear their charges; that by this means acts for money, importation of French wine, and the like, may pass in a thin house, which will not fail immediately to receive the royal assent, whilst the acts that concern the welfare, and perhaps the very being of the nation, remain untouched.

XI

My Lord Chancellor

Being under some apprehensions that her Majesty may receive ill advice in this affair, from ministers who frequently mistake former bad practices for good precedents, I desire that the third act of the first session of the first parliament of King Charles the second may be read.

Act the third of the first session, parl. I. Car. II.

Act asserting his Majesty's royal prerogative, in calling and dissolving of parliaments, and making of laws.

The estates of parliament now convened by his Majesty's special authority, considering that the quietness, stability, and happiness of the people, do depend upon the safety of the King's Majesty's sacred person, and the maintenance of his sovereign authority, princely power, and prerogative royal; and conceiving themselves obliged in conscience, and in discharge of their duties to almighty God, to the King's Majesty, and to their native country, to make a due acknowledgment thereof at this time, do therefore unanimously declare, that they will with their lives and fortunes maintain and defend the same. And they do hereby acknowledge, that the power of calling, holding, proroguing, and dissolving of parliaments, and all conventions and meetings of the estates, does solely reside in the King's Majesty, his heirs, and successors. And that as no parliament can be lawfully kept, without the special warrant and presence of the King's Majesty, or his Commissioner; so no acts, sentences, or statutes, to be passed in parliament, can be binding upon the people, or have the authority and force of laws, without the special authority and approbation of the King's Majesty, or his Commissioner interponed thereto, at the making thereof. And therefore the King's Majesty, with advice and consent of his estates of parliament, doth hereby rescind and annul all laws, acts, statutes, or practices that have been, or upon any pretext whatsoever may be, or seem contrary to, or inconsistent with, his Majesty's just power and prerogative above-mentioned; and declares the same to have been unlawful, and to be void and null in all time coming. And to the end that this act and acknowledgment, which the estates of parliament, from the sense of their humble duty

87

and certain knowledge, have hereby made, may receive the more exact obedi-
ence in time coming; it is by his Majesty, with advice foresaid, statute and
ordained, that the punctual observance thereof be specially regarded by all
his Majesty's subjects, and that none of them, upon any pretext whatsoever,
offer to call in question, impugn, or do any deed to the contrary hereof, under
pain of treason.

My Lord Chancellor

The questions concerning the King's prerogative and the people's privileges are nice and difficult. Mr. William Colvin, who was one of the wisest men this nation ever had, used to say concerning defensive arms, that he wished all princes thought them lawful, and the people unlawful. And indeed I heartily wish that something like these moderate sentiments might always determine all matters in question between both. By the constitution of this kingdom, no act of the estates had the force of a law, unless touched by the King's sceptre, which was his undoubted prerogative. The touch of his sceptre gave authority to our laws, as his stamp did a currency to our coin: but he had no right to refuse or withhold either. It is pretended by some men, that in virtue of this act, the King may refuse the royal assent to acts passed by the estates of the kingdom. But it ought to be considered, that this law is only an acknowledgment and declaration of the King's prerogative, and consequently gives nothing new to the prince. The act acknowledges this to be the prerogative of the King, that whatever is passed in this house, cannot have the force of a law without the royal assent, and makes it high treason to question this prerogative; because the parliament, during the civil war, had usurped a power of imposing their own votes upon the people for law, though neither the King, nor any person commissionated by him were present: and this new law was wholly and simply directed to abolish and rescind that usurpation, as appears by the tenor and express words of the act; which does neither acknowledge nor declare, that the prince has a power to refuse the royal assent to any act presented by the parliament. If any one should say that the lawgivers designed no less, and that the principal contrivers and promoters of the act frequently boasted they had obtained the negative, as they call it, for the crown, I desire to know how they will make that appear, since no words are to be found in the act, that show any such design: especially if we consider, that this law was made by a parliament that spoke the most plainly, least equivocally, and most fully of all others concerning the prerogative. And if those who promoted the passing of this act were under so strong a delusion, to think they had obtained a new and great prerogative to the crown by a declaratory law, in which there is not one word to that purpose, it was the hand of heaven that defeated their design of destroying the liberty of their country. I know our princes have refused their assent to some acts since the making of this law: but a practice introduced in arbitrary times can deserve no consideration. For my own part, I am far from pushing things to extremity on either hand: I heartily enter into the sentiments of the wise man I mentioned before, and think the people of this nation might have been happy in mistaking the meaning of this law, if such men as have had the greatest credit with our princes would have let them into the true sense of it. And therefore those who have the honour to advise her Majesty should beware of inducing her to a refusal of the royal assent to the act for the security of the kingdom, because the unwarrantable custom of rejecting acts was introduced in arbitrary times.

XII

My Lord Chancellor

It is often said in this house, that parliaments, and especially long sessions of parliament, are a heavy tax and burden to this nation: I suppose they mean as things are usually managed: otherwise I should think it a great reflection on the wisdom of the nation, and a maxim very pernicious to our government. But indeed in the present state of things, they are a very great burden to us. Our parliament seldom meets in winter, when the season of the year and our own private affairs bring us to town. We are called together for the most part in summer, when our country business and the goodness of the season make us live in town with regret. Our parliaments are sitting both in seed-time and harvest, and we are made to toil the whole year. We meet one day in three; though no reason can be given why we should not meet every day, unless such a one, as I am unwilling to name, lest thereby occasion should be taken to mention it elsewhere to the reproach of the nation. The expenses of our commissioners are now become greater than those of our kings formerly were: and a great part of this money is laid out upon equipage and other things of foreign manufacture, to the great damage of the kingdom. We meet in this place in the afternoon, after a great dinner, which I think is not the time of doing business; and are in such confusion after the candles are lighted, that very often the debate of one single point cannot be finished, but must be put off to another day. Parliaments are forced to submit to the conveniences of the lords of the session, and meetings of the burghs; though no good reason can be given, why either a lord of the session or any one deputed to the meetings of the burghs, should be a member of this house; but on the contrary, experience has taught us the inconvenience of both. When members of parliament, to perform the duty they owe to their country, have left the most important affairs, and quitted their friends many times in the utmost extremity, to be present at this place, they are told they may return again; as we were the other day called together only in order to be dismissed. We have been for several days adjourned in this time of harvest, when we had the most important affairs under deliberation; that as well those who have neither place nor pension might grow weary of their attendance, as those, whose ill state of health makes the service of their country as dangerous, though no less honourable than if they served in the field. Do not these things show us the necessity of those limitations, I had the honour to offer to this house? and particularly of that for lodging the power of adjournments in the parliament; that for meetings of parliament to be in winter; that for empowering the President to give the royal assent, and ascertaining his salary; with that for excluding all lords of the session from being members of parliament. Could one imagine that in this parliament, in which we have had the first opportunity of amending our constitution by new conditions of government, occasion should be given by reiterating former abuses, to convince all men of the necessity of farther limitations upon a successor? Or is not this rather to be attributed to a peculiar providence, that those who are the great opposers of limitations should by their conduct give the best reason for them? But I hope no member of this house will be discouraged either by delay or opposition; because the liberties of a people are not to be maintained without passing through great difficulties, and that no toil and labours ought to be declined to preserve a nation from slavery.

XIII

My Lord Chancellor

I have waited long and with great patience for the result of this session, to see if I could discover a real and sincere intention in the members of this house to restore the freedom of our country in this great and perhaps only opportunity. I know there are many different views among us, and all men pretend the good of the nation. But every man here is obliged carefully to examine the things before us, and to act according to his knowledge and conscience, without regard to the views of other men, whatever charity he may have for them: I say, every man in this place is obliged by the oath he has taken to give such advice as he thinks most expedient for the good of his country. The principal business of this session has been the forming of an act for the security of the kingdom, upon the expiration of the present entail of the crown. And though one would have thought that the most essential thing which could have entered into such an act, had been to ascertain the conditions on which the nation would receive a successor, yet this has been entirely waived and over-ruled by the house. Only there is a caution inserted in the act, that the successor shall not be the same person who is to succeed in England, unless such conditions of government be first enacted as may secure the freedom of this nation. But this is a general and indefinite clause, and liable to the dangerous inconveniency of being declared to be fulfilled by giving us two or three inconsiderable laws. So that this session of parliament, in which we have had so great an opportunity of making ourselves for ever a free people, is like to terminate without any real security for our liberties, or any essential amendment of our constitution. And now, when we ought to come to particulars, and enact such limitations as may fully satisfy the general clause, we must amuse ourselves with things of little significancy, and hardly mention any limitation of moment or consequence. But instead of this, acts are brought in for regulations to take place during the life of the Queen, which we are not to expect, and quite draw us off from the business we should attend. By these methods divers well-meaning men have been deluded, whilst others have proposed a present nomination of a successor under limitations. But I fear the far greater part have designed to make their court either to her Majesty, the house of Hanover, or those of St. Germains, by maintaining the prerogative in Scotland as high as ever, to the perpetual enslaving of this nation to the ministers of England. Therefore I, who have never made court to any prince, and I hope never shall, at the rate of the least prejudice to my country, think myself obliged in discharge of my conscience, and the duty of my oath in parliament, to offer such limitations as may answer the general clause in the act for the security of the kingdom. And this I do in two draughts, the one containing the limitations by themselves; the other with the same limitations, and a blank for inserting the name of a successor. If the house shall think fit to take into consideration that draught which has no blank, and enact the limitations, I shall rest satisfied, being as little fond of naming a successor as any man. Otherwise, I offer the draught with a blank; to the end that every man may make his court to the person he most affects; and hope by this means to please all parties: the court in offering them an opportunity to name the successor of England, a thing so acceptable to her Majesty and that nation: those who may favour the court of St. Germains, by giving them a chance for their pretensions; and every true Scotsman, in vindicating the liberty of this nation, whoever be the successor.

First Draught

Our sovereign Lady, with advice and consent of the estates of parliament, statutes and ordains, that after the decease of her Majesty (whom God long preserve) and failing heirs of her body, no one shall succeed to the crown of this realm that is likewise successor to the crown of England, but under the limitations following, which, together with the oath of coronation and claim of right, they shall swear to observe. That all places and offices, both civil and military, and all pensions formerly conferred by our kings, shall ever after be given by parliament.—That a new parliament shall be chosen every Michaelmas head-court, to sit the first of November thereafter, and adjourn themselves from time to time till next Michaelmas; and that they choose their own president.—That a committee of thirty-six members, chosen by and out of the whole parliament, without distinction of estates, shall, during the intervals of parliament, under the king, have the administration of the government, be his council, and accountable to parliament; with power, in extraordinary occasions, to call the parliament together.

Second Draught

Our sovereign Lady, with advice and consent of the estates of parliament, statutes and ordains, that after the decease of her Majesty (whom God long preserve) and heirs of her body failing,

                              shall succeed to the crown of this realm.
But that in case the said successor be likewise the successor to the crown of England, the said successor shall be under the limitations following, &c.

No man can be an enemy to these limitations, in case we have the same king with England, except he who is so shameless a partisan either of the court of St. Germains, or the house of Hanover, that he would rather see Scotland continue to depend upon an English ministry, than that their prerogative should be any way lessened in this kingdom. As for those who have St. Germains in their view, and are accounted the highest of all the prerogative-men, I would ask them, if we should assist them in advancing their Prince to the throne of Great Britain, are we, for our reward, to continue still in our former dependence on the English court? These limitations are the only test to discover a lover of his country from a courtier either to her Majesty, Hanover, or St. Germains. For prerogative-men who are for enslaving this nation to the directions of another court, are courtiers to any successor; and let them pretend what they will, if their principles lead necessarily to subject this nation to another, are enemies to the nation. These men are so absurd as to provoke England, and yet resolve to continue slaves of that court. This country must be made a field of blood, in order to advance a papist to the throne of Britain. If we fail, we shall be slaves by right of conquest; if we prevail, have the happiness to continue in our former slavish dependence. And though to break this yoke all good men would venture their all, yet I believe few will be willing to lie at the mercy of France and popery, and at the same time draw upon themselves the indignation and power of England, for the sake only of measuring our strength with a much more powerful nation; and to be sure to continue still under our former dependence, though we should happen to prevail. Now of those who are for the same successor with England, I would ask, if in that case we are not also to continue in our former dependence; which will not fail always to grow from bad to worse, and at length become more intolerable to all honest men than death itself. For my own part I think, that even the most zealous protestant in the nation, if he have a true regard for his country, ought rather to wish (were it consistent with our claim of right) that a papist should succeed to the throne of Great Britain under such limitations as would render this nation free and independent, than the most protestant and best prince, without any. If we may live free, I little value who is king: it is indifferent to me, provided the limitations be enacted, to name or not name; Hanover, St. Germains, or whom you will.

XIV

My Lord Chancellor

His grace the high Commissioner having acquainted this house that he has instructions from her Majesty to give the royal assent to all acts passed in this session, except that for the security of the kingdom, it will be highly necessary to provide some new laws for securing our liberty upon the expiration of the present entail of the crown. And therefore I shall speak to the first article of the limitations contained in the short act I offered the other day; not only because it is the first in order, but because I persuade myself you all know that parliaments were formerly chosen annually; that they had the power of appointing the times of their meetings and adjournments, together with the nomination of committees to superintend the administration of the government during the intervals of parliament: all which, if it were necessary, might be proved by a great number of public acts. So that if I demonstrate the use and necessity of the first article, there will remain no great difficulty concerning the rest.

My Lord Chancellor

The condition of a people, however unhappy, if they not only know the cause of their misery, but have also the remedy in their power, and yet should refuse to apply it, one would think, were not to be pitied. And though the condition of good men, who are concluded and oppressed by a majority of the bad, is much to be lamented; yet Christianity teaches us to show a greater measure of compassion to those who are knowingly and voluntarily obstinate to ruin both themselves and others. But the regret of every wise and good man must needs be extraordinary, when he sees the liberty and happiness of his country not only obstructed, but utterly extinguished by the private and transitory interest of self-designing men, who indeed very often meet their own ruin, but most certainly bring destruction upon their posterity by such courses. Sure if a man who is entrusted by others, should for his own private advantage betray that trust, to the perpetual and irrecoverable ruin of those who trusted him, the liveliest sense and deepest remorse for so great guilt, will undoubtedly seize and terrify the conscience of such a man, as often as the treacherous part he has acted shall recur to his thoughts; which will most frequently happen in the times of his distress, and the nearer he approaches to a life in which those remorses are perpetual. But I hope every man in this house has so well considered these things, as to preserve him from falling into such terrible circumstances: and (as all men are subject to great failings) if any person placed in this most eminent trust is conscious to himself of having ever been wanting in duty to his country, I doubt not he will this day, in this weighty matter, atone for all, and not blindly follow the opinion of other men, because he alone must account for his own actions to his great Lord and Master.

The limitation, to which I am about to speak, requires, that all places, offices, and pensions, which have been formerly given by our kings, shall, after her Majesty and heirs of her body, be conferred by parliament so long as we are under the same prince with England. Without this limitation, our poverty and subjection to the court of England will every day increase; and the question we have now before us is, whether we will be freemen or slaves for ever? whether we will continue to depend, or break the yoke of our dependence? and whether we will choose to live poor and miserable, or rich, free, and happy? Let no man think to object that this limitation takes away the whole power of the prince. For the same condition of government is found in one of the most absolute monarchies of the world. I have very good authority for what I say, from all the best authors that have treated of the government of China; but shall only cite the words of an able minister of state, who had very well considered whatever had been written on that subject; I mean Sir William Temple, who says, 'That for the government, it is absolute monarchy, there being no other laws in China, but the King's orders and commands; and it is likewise hereditary, still descending to the next of blood. But all orders and commands of the King proceed through his councils; and are made upon the recommendation or petition of the council proper and appointed for that affair: so that all matters are debated, determined, and concluded by the several councils; and then upon their advices and requests made to the King, they are ratified and signed by him, and so pass into laws. All great offices of state are likewise conferred by the King, upon the same recommendations or petitions of his several councils; so that none are preferred by the humour of the prince himself, nor by favour of any minister, by flattery or corruption, but by the force or appearance of merit, of learning, and of virtue; which observed by the several councils, gain their recommendations or petitions to the King.' These are the express words of that minister. And if under the greatest absolute monarchy of the world, in a country where the prince actually resides; if among heathens this be accounted a necessary part of government for the encouragement of virtue, shall it be denied to Christians living under a prince who resides in another nation? Shall it be denied to a people, who have a right to liberty, and yet are not capable of any in their present circumstances, without this limitation? But we have formed to ourselves such extravagant notions of government, that even in a limited monarchy nothing will please, which in the least deviates from the model of France, and everything else must stand branded with the name of commonwealth. Yet a great and wise people found this very condition of government necessary to support even an absolute monarchy. If any man say that the empire of China contains divers kingdoms; and that the care of the Emperor, and his knowledge of particular men cannot extend to all: I answer, the case is the same with us; and it seems as if that wise people designed this constitution for a remedy to the like inconveniences with those we labour under at this time.

This limitation will undoubtedly enrich the nation, by stopping that perpetual issue of money to England, which has reduced this country to extreme poverty. This limitation does not flatter us with the hopes of riches by an uncertain project; does not require so much as the condition of our own industry; but by saving great sums to the country, will every year furnish a stock sufficient to carry on a considerable trade, or to establish some useful manufacture at home, with the highest probability of success: because our ministers by this rule of government would be freed from the influence of English councils; and our trade be entirely in our own hands, and not under the power of the court, as it was in the affair of Darien. If we do not obtain this limitation, our attendance at London will continue to drain this nation of all those sums, which should be a stock for trade. Besides, by frequenting that court, we not only spend our money, but learn the expensive modes and ways of living, of a rich and luxurious nation: we lay out yearly great sums in furniture and equipage, to the unspeakable prejudice of the trade and manufactures of our own country. Not that I think it amiss to travel into England, in order to see and learn their industry in trade and husbandry. But at court what can we learn, except a horrid corruption of manners, and an expensive way of living, that we may for ever after be both poor and profligate?

This limitation will secure to us our freedom and independence. It has been often said in this house that our princes are captives in England; and indeed one would not wonder if, when our interest happens to be different from that of England, our kings, who must be supported by the riches and power of that nation in all their undertakings, should prefer an English interest before that of this country. It is yet less strange, that English ministers should advise and procure the advancement of such persons to the ministry of Scotland, as will comply with their measures and the King's orders; and to surmount the difficulties they may meet with from a true Scots interest, that places and pensions should be bestowed upon parliament-men and others: I say, these things are so far from wonder, that they are inevitable in the present state of our affairs. But I hope they likewise show us that we ought not to continue any longer in this condition. Now this limitation is advantageous to all. The prince will no more be put upon the hardship of deciding between an English and a Scots interest; or the difficulty of reconciling what he owes to each nation, in consequence of his coronation oath. Even English ministers will no longer lie under the temptation of meddling in Scots affairs: nor the ministers of this kingdom, together with all those who have places and pensions, be any more subject to the worst of all slavery. But if the influences I mentioned before shall still continue, what will any other limitation avail us? What shall we be the better for our act concerning the power of war and peace, since by the force of an English interest and influence, we cannot fail of being engaged in every way, and neglected in every peace?

By this limitation, our parliament will become the most uncorrupted senate of all Europe. No man will be tempted to vote against the interest of his country, when his country shall have all the bribes in her own hands: offices, places, pensions. It will be no longer necessary to lose one half of the public customs, that parliament-men may be made collectors. We will not desire to exclude the officers of state from sitting in this house, when the country shall have the nomination of them; and our parliaments free from corruption cannot fail to redress all our grievances. We shall then have no cause to fear a refusal of the royal assent to our acts; for we shall have no evil counsellor, nor enemy of his country to advise it. When this condition of government shall take place, the royal assent will be the ornament of the prince, and never be refused to the desires of the people. A general unanimity will be found in this house; in every part of the government, and among all ranks and conditions of men. The distinctions of court and country-party shall no more be heard in this nation; nor shall the prince and people any longer have a different interest. Rewards and punishments will be in the hands of those who live among us, and consequently best know the merit of men; by which means virtue will be recompensed and vice discouraged, and the reign and government of the prince will flourish in peace and justice.

I should never make an end, if I would proseeute all the great advantages of this limitation; which, like a divine influence, turns all to good, as the want of it has hitherto poisoned everything, and brought all to ruin. I shall therefore only add one particular more, in which it will be of the highest advantage to this nation. We all know, that the only way of enslaving a people is by keeping up a standing army; that by standing forces all limited monarchies have been destroyed, without them none; that so long as any standing forces are allowed in a nation, pretexts will never be wanting to increase them; that princes have never suffered militias to be put upon any good foot, lest standing forces should appear unnecessary. We also know that a good and well-regulated militia is of so great importance to a nation, as to be the principal part of the constitution of any free government. Now by this limitation, the nation will have a sufficient power to render their militia good and effectual, by the nomination of officers: and if we would send a certain proportion of our militia abroad yearly, and relieve them from time to time, we may make them as good as those of Switzerland are; and much more able to defend the country, than any unactive standing forces can be. We may save every year great sums of money, which are now expended to maintain a standing army; and which is yet more, run no hazard of losing our liberty by them. We may employ a greater number of officers in those detachments, than we do at present in all our forces both at home and abroad; and make better conditions for them in those countries that need their assistance. For being freed from the influences of English councils, we shall certainly look better than we have hitherto done to the terms on which we may send them into the armies either of England or Holland; and not permit them to be abused so many different ways, as to the great reproach of the nation they have been, in their rank, pay, clothing, arrears, levy-money, quarters, transport ships, and gratuities.

Having thus shown some of the great advantages this limitation will bring to the nation (to which everyone of you will be able to add many more) that it is not only consistent with monarchy, but even with an absolute monarchy; having demonstrated the necessity of such a condition in all empires, which contain several kingdoms; and that without it we must for ever continue in a dependence upon the court of England; in the name of God, what hinders us from embracing so great a blessing? Is it because her Majesty will refuse the royal assent to this act? If she do, sure I am, such a refusal must proceed from the advice of English counsellors; and will not that be a demonstration to us, that after her Majesty and heirs of her body, we must not, cannot any longer continue under the same prince with England? Shall we be wanting to ourselves? Can her Majesty give her assent to this limitation upon a successor before you offer it to her? Is she at liberty to give us satisfaction in this point, till we have declared to England by a vote of this house, that unless we obtain this condition, we will not name the same successor with them? And then will not her Majesty, even by English advice, be persuaded to give her assent; unless her counsellors shall think fit to incur the heavy imputation, and run the dangerous risk of dividing these nations for ever? If therefore either reason, honour, or conscience have any influence upon us; if we have any regard either to ourselves or posterity; if there be any such thing as virtue, happiness, or reputation in this world, or felicity in a future state, let me adjure you by all these, not to draw upon your heads everlasting infamy, attended with the eternal reproaches and anguish of an evil conscience, by making yourselves and your posterity miserable.

XV

My Lord Chancellor

This is an act for repealing a law made in the year 1700, which prohibits the importation of French wines. We were then in peace with France, and are now in a declared war against them. The prohibition was made in time of peace, because the French laid greater impositions upon our trade than they did upon other nations: and yet it is desired that French wines may be imported in time of war; though not only the same, but new burdens are laid upon our merchandise in France. It is pretended that we shall not trade to France directly, but may buy French wines from certain nations who trade to that country with our goods. I will allow all this, though it be false; but where is the necessity we should take French wines from those nations for our commodities? Have they not copper, iron, pitch, tar, hemp, flax, and timber for building of ships and other uses, which we need? or if our consumption of these things will not answer the value of those goods they take of us, may we not export the overplus to other parts? Since therefore the same or greater impositions continue still upon our merchandise in France, so as we cannot get of those neutral nations so high a price for our goods, as if the impositions in France were taken off, the reason of the law made in 1700 still remains. And if we had sufficient cause to prohibit the importation of French wines by our own ships in time of peace, shall we purchase French wines from other nations in time of war? The French would not receive our goods in time of peace, upon equal terms with those of other nations, which obliged us to forbid their wines: shall we now take them at a double value in time of war? or are we become greater friends to France now in a time of open war, than we were before in time of peace? Something might be said, if no wines were to be found in Portugal or Italy. But it seems no wine will please us, but that of a country, against which we are in actual war, and which uses us ill both in peace and war. One would have thought that the past services of a nation, which has more than once saved that base people from ruin, might have obliged them to a more favourable usage of us. But the world will say, we are yet a baser people than they, if whilst they continue to suppress our trade, we repeal a law, for which we have now more and better reasons than when we made it. To repeal such a law in time of war will found admirably well in England and Holland: since it is no less than a direct breach of our alliance with those nations; a formal renunciation of any advantages we may pretend in a treaty of peace, and exactly calculated to inform the world of the inclinations of our ministers. If we would trade to Portugal and Italy, we should have the benefit of English and Dutch convoys. We might trade in our own ships, not in Swedes, Danes, and Hamburghers, to the ruin of our navigation. For if they drive our trade for us, we may indeed burn our ships and plough our towns, as has been told us. And therefore I move that this act, as prejudicial to our trade and navigation, and highly injurious to the honour of the nation, may be thrown out.

XVI

My Lord Chancellor

One would think that of all men law-givers should be of the most undoubted probity, and that selfish ends and disingenuity should have no place in their assemblies. For if those who give laws to other men have not the good of the nations they govern in view, but are ready to sacrifice everything to their own private interest, such a scandalous conduct must be of the last consequence to a government, by alienating the affections of the people from those who shall be found guilty of such practices. My Lord, no man in this house can be ignorant that this act will not only open a trade and correspondence with France, contrary to the declaration of war, and our own standing laws; but that the design of those who promote the passing of this act is to have a trade directly with France. It is known that Scots ships are already loading wines at Bourdeaux for this kingdom; and that a French factor is already arrived in this city. Besides, it is notorious, that a ship belonging to this port, and freighted with wines from France, is now lying in Queensferry-road, not eight miles from this place. She pretends indeed to be a Dane, because she came last from Norway; whither she was sent for no other reason than that she came too soon upon this coast. This ship has an officer and divers seamen on board, sent from one of our frigates for her guard, who have absolutely refused to permit the persons that were empowered by the admiralty to examine her, unless they should produce an order from the captain of the frigate, or from your lordship. And as if our act for the prohibition of French wines were already repealed, and our collectors, no less than our former kings, might dispense with the laws, another ship laden with the wines of that country has been brought into the Clyde, and her lading into the city of Glasgow, during this session, in contempt of the law and the authority of the parliament. All this, and much more of the same kind, is well known to those who are in the administration, and seem not to think it their business to take notice of such practices. But I hope this house will not overlook these gross mismanagements; and since the executive part of the government is arrived to that state, that hardly any law is put in execution, the parliament, according to the many precedents we have in our acts, will give order for a better administration in time to come, and take effectual care that those who are placed in the highest trusts shall see the laws duly executed; especially your lordship, who during the intervals of parliament, as the principal person in the government, ought to be answerable to the nation for their due execution. Now the great argument which is used for allowing the importation of French wines is, that we shall certainly have the wines of that country, though very bad and very dear, if the prohibition be continued. Which is only to say, we have no government among us. Two good laws were made in the year 1700. One against the exportation of our wool, the other against the importation of French wines; the first to give a being to a woollen manufacture in this kingdom, the latter to vindicate our trade against the impositions of France. We have already rendered the one ineffectual, to the ruin of our woollen manufacture; shall we now repeal the other? Shall we send them our wool, and buy their wines, and oblige them doubly for burdening and oppressing us in our trade? It is pretended that the customs arising from the importation of French wines must serve to pay the civil list, because the former duties are fallen one half of the usual value. A very cogent argument indeed! when we know that the customs have been taken from the farmers, only in order to bestow the collectors' places upon parliament-men. Shall we make good such funds as are exhausted by bribing men to betray our liberty? If any justice were to be found in this nation, the advisers of these things had long since been brought to a scaffold. But as there is no crime under heaven more enormous, more treacherous, and more destructive to the very nature of our government, than that of bribing parliaments; so there is nothing more common and barefaced: and I think this session should have been opened by purging the house from such corrupted members; which if we had done, we had not met with so many difficulties and obstructions of the public service. But I hope we shall not be so remiss for the future. And for the present, my Lord Chancellor, I move, that this act for taking off the prohibition of French wines, as a design of the blackest nature, hurtful and ignominious to the nation, and highly reflecting on our ministers and administration, may be thrown out.

XVII

My Lord Chancellor

Yesterday a cause was brought into this house by a protestation for remeid of law: upon which a debate arose, whether a lord of session, who is also a member of this house for some shire or burgh, could sit again as a judge of the same cause. I was then of opinion he might; because the house had declared they would not confine themselves to decide this matter by what had been already alleged and proved before the lords of session; but would receive new proof and matter, if any had been discovered since the passing of the decreet. And indeed in that case I was of opinion those lords of session might and ought to judge again, because new proof and new matter might induce them to alter their former judgment. But since no new matter or proof appears, and that the vote is stated, 'Adhere to the decreet of the lords of session, or sustain the protestation'; which is only and simply to determine the cause by what was alleged and proved before that bench; I cannot consent that any of those lords, though members of this house, should again be judges of the same cause. Nor indeed, till the house had over-ruled my opinion, could I think that we ought to decide any cause brought before us by protestation for remeid of law, otherwise than by the proofs and matters alleged and proved before the lords of session. Certainly it was never designed, by allowing these protestations, to bring all civil causes before our parliaments. For if we should judge of matters originally in this house, or go about to redress and relieve men against their adversaries upon new proof after the decreet of the ordinary judges, all the civil causes of the nation might under one pretext or another be brought before us. In these cases we are only to relieve the people by reversing the unjust sentences of the lords of session. And the privilege of the people to protest for remeid of law was principally designed to be a check upon the ordinary judges, and oblige them to do justice: which if they should not do, and were convicted of bribery or other gross injustice, the parliament might remove them from their offices, or otherwise punish them in life or estate. So that these lords of session, who have formerly determined this cause, cannot, I think, reasonably pretend to judge the same again, though they are members of the house; because no man can be judge of anything by which he may receive damage or profit. If the decreet now under consideration shall be found grossly unjust, I hope no man will say the judges may not be punished. And the judgment to be given by the parliament is to be confined to this; whether the lords of session have pronounced a just or unjust sentence. In the giving of which judgment, no lord of session can be present as judge; unless we will say that an unjust judge may be absolved by his own vote. But to all this a very easy remedy is to be found; I mean, that no lord of session should be a member of parliament, which would be highly advantageous to the nation on many accounts, and principally that our parliaments might no longer interrupt or disturb the common course of justice.

These speeches are published to prevent mistakes in the affairs to which they relate.

An ACCOUNT of

A CONVERSATION

CONCERNING

A RIGHT REGULATION

O F

GOVERNMENTS

For the common Good of Mankind.

I N

A LETTER to the Marquiſs of
Montrose, the Earls of Rothes,
Roxburg and Haddington,

From London the firſt of December, 1703.

Edinburgh;
Printed in the Year MDCCIV.

AN ACCOUNT OF A
CONVERSATION &c.

My Lords

You desire to know the sentiments of some considerable persons of the
English nation, touching our affairs, and the common interest of both
kingdoms. And I think I cannot give you more satisfaction in these
particulars than by an account of a conversation I lately had with the
Earl of Cr–m–rty, Sir Ed. S—m–r, and Sir Chr. M-sgr-ve; in which if
the defence I made for you do not give you satisfaction, I shall be glad
to hear a better from yourselves. If you ask how I had the fortune to
meet with men of sentiments so different from my own, that was partly
owing to chance, and partly to the frank and courteous way which is so
natural to the Earl of Cr–m–rty. For some days ago, walking slowly and
alone in the Mall, the Earl and Sir Chr-st-ph-r overtook me: and
though during the whole time I was last in Scotland, I had not waited
on the Earl, he with a very obliging air said to me, that if I expected
not other company, they would be glad of mine; asking me withal if
I was acquainted with Sir Chr. I said I had formerly the honour of
some small acquaintance with him, which I should be very willing to
renew. And after some compliments passed on all sides, finding I was
not engaged, he invited me to dine with him, telling me he would give
me the opportunity of doing as I desired; and therefore we should pass
the time together till the hour of dinner. So we presently went to his
lodging in Whitehall, and entering into a room from whence we had a
full view of the Thames and city of London. You have here, gentlemen,
said the Earl, two of the noblest objects that can entertain the eye, the
finest river, and the greatest city in the world. Where natural things
are in the greatest perfection, they never fail to produce most wonderful effects. This most gentle and navigable river, with the excellent
genius and industrious inclination of the English people, have raised
this glorious city to such a height, that if all things be rightly considered, we shall find it very far to surpass any other. Besides the beauty
and conveniences of the river, the situation of this city is such, that I

am persuaded if the wisest men of the nation had been many years employed to choose the most advantageous, they could not have found a better: and as the prosperity of a country depends in a great measure upon the situation of the capital city, the good fortune of this nation in that particular, has chiefly contributed to the great riches and power they now have. My lord, said Sir Chr—, you are so fully in the right, that notwithstanding the extent, and particularly the great length of the buildings; yet should they be removed but one half-mile either east or west, such an alteration would be disadvantageous. For to the eastward some rows of buildings do in a straight line cross the fields, and meet the river again at Blackwall; and to the westward the buildings run along a rising ground which overlooks Hyde Park, and the adjacent fields. The whole town lies upon a shelving situation, descending easily, and as it were in the form of a theatre towards the south and river, covered from the north, northeast, and northwest winds: so that in very cold and stormy weather, by means of the buildings of the city and on the bridge, it is both warm and calm upon the river; which being as it were the string to the bow, affords the great conveniency of a cheap and speedy conveyance from one part to the other. The shelving situation of the city is not only most fitted to receive the kind influences of the sun, but to carry off by common-shores and other ways the snow and dirt of the streets into the river, which is cleansed by the tides twice every day. But above all, the ground on which the city stands being a gravel, renders the inhabitants healthful, and the adjacent country wholesome and beautiful. The county of Kent furnishes us with the choicest fruit; Hertfordshire and Cambridgeshire with corn; Lincolnshire, Essex, and Surrey with beef, veal, and mutton; Buckinghamshire with wood for fuel; and the river with all that the seas and the rest of the world affords. And this in so great plenty, that in times of peace, the common fuel, though brought two hundred miles by sea, is yet sold at a reasonable rate; and in so great variety, that we may find more sorts of wine in London than in the countries which produce the richest and the most. In a word, all the useful and superfluous things that nature produces, or the wit of man has invented, are to be found here, either made by our artificers, or imported by our merchants. That which is to be admired, said I, is the perfect peace and tranquillity in which the inhabitants live; proceeding either from their natural temper, or the good order and plenty of the place, and the security they enjoy from the attempts of any enemy by being situated in an island. So that this great city without walls or guards is as accessible at all hours of the night as the most inconsiderable village. But that which charms me most is the liberty and rights they are possessed of in matters civil and religious. To these advantages I might add many things which render this city great, convenient, and agreeable; such are: the important transactions of a parliament; the judgments in Westminster Hall; the business of the Exchange, navigation, and commerce; the affairs and diversions of the court, together with the recreations and pleasures of the town. These last words have spoiled all, said Sir Chr., and unluckily revived in me the image of that corruption of manners which reigns in this place, has infected the whole nation, and must at length bring both the city and nation to ruin. And if one may judge by the greatness of the corruption, this fatal period is not far off. For no regulations of government are sufficient to restrain or correct the manners of so great a number of people living in one place, and exposed to so many temptations from the bad example they give to one another. And the frequency of ill example, which can never fail to be where so great numbers live together, authorizes the corruption, and will always be too strong and powerful for any magistracy to control. For though every man may have his own scheme to reform and regulate these disorders, yet experience has taught us that no human prudence can preserve the manners of men living in great cities from extraordinary corruption; and that where great power, riches, and numbers of men are brought together, they not only introduce a universal depravation of manners, but destroy all good government, and bring ruin and desolation upon a people. What great corruptions do you find in this place, so obstinate and incorrigible? said the Earl. No laws or regulations, replied Sir Chr—, are sufficient to restrain the luxury of women, to banish so many thousands of common prostitutes, or to prevent a far greater number of that sex from being debauched by the innumerable occasions and opportunities which so vast a city affords, where by means of a masque, a hackney-coach, a tavern, and a play-house, they are at liberty to do what they please. Even the poorer sort of both sexes are daily tempted to all manner of lewdness by infamous ballads sung in every corner of the streets. One would think, said the Earl, this last were of no great consequence. I said, I knew a very wise man so much of Sir Chr—'s sentiment, that he believed if a man were permitted to make all the ballads, he need not care who should make the laws of a nation. And we find that most of the ancient legislators thought they could not well reform the manners of any city without the help of a lyric, and sometimes of a dramatic poet. But in

108

this city the dramatic poet no less than the ballad-maker has been almost wholly employed to corrupt the people, in which they have had most unspeakable and deplorable success. Then Sir Chr— continuing his discourse, said, in this city gamesters, stockjobbers, jockys, and wagerers make now the most considerable figure, and in few years have attained to such a degree of perfection in their several ways, that in comparison to many of the nobility, gentry, and merchants of England, those in Newgate are mere ignorants, and wretches of no experience. In the summer they infest all the places of diversion throughout England, and may be justly called the missioners of this city. Sure, said the Earl, remedies may be found for many of these abuses. The too expensive apparel of women might be restrained, masques might be prohibited; vinters forbidden to receive women in their houses, and all stockjobbing, gaming, and wagering suppressed. But who, said Sir Chr—, is to do this? for though these things might be easily done in a small city, yet in this place I am confident that the authority of the Queen and parliament would not be found sufficient for such a performance. I am fully persuaded of her Majesty's sincere intentions to discourage vice; yet some wise counsellor will not fail to tell her that it would be of dangerous consequence to forbid gaming, which consumes so much of the time, and takes up the thoughts of a great number of men, who, if they had not that diversion, might probably employ their leisure in thinking too much upon affairs of state. Might not we, said the Earl, play, like the Turks, only to pass the time? No, replied Sir Chr—, you have to do with Christians, who have a Christian liberty to play for money, provided they do not abuse it; though all men know, that if the thing be allowed, the abuse is inevitable. And yet this is not the worst; for the infection of bad manners has so thoroughly corrupted this place, that many even of those who ought by wholesome laws to reform others, are themselves infected by the contagion; so that when the country has sent persons to represent them in parliament, they in a short time seem rather to be the only representatives of this corrupt city, and artfully betray the nation, under the fairest pretences to good principles, contrary to their known duty, and the important trust reposed in them. I said, Sir Chr—'s observations were very impartial, and that I wished all those who were guilty of such practices, would impartially apply so just a censure to themselves. Sir Chr— continuing, said: all abuses, when introduced among great multitudes, become not only more enormous, but more incorrigible. The justices of London and Westminster will inform you of a thousand evils and incorrigible practices, which wholly proceed from the great number of the inhabitants and vast extent of our buildings, where all manner of crimes are easily concealed. Besides, the poor and indigent are so numerous in this place, that the ill practices to which men are tempted by poverty, are but too frequent: and the luxury of all other ranks and orders of men makes every one hasten to grow rich; and consequently leads them to betray all kind of trust reposed in them. In a word, this city abounds with all manner of temptations to evil; extreme poverty, excessive riches, great pleasures, infinite bad examples, especially of unpunished and successful crimes. Here Sir Chr— was interrupted by a servant, who acquainted us that Sir Ed. S—m-r was coming upstairs. He is welcome, said the Earl; and the more because he comes so early, for I expected him not until the hour of dinner. Upon this Sir Edw-rd S-m-r entered the room, and after he had saluted the Earl and Sir Chr—, the Earl presented me as his countryman and old acquaintance to Sir Edw-rd; and when we had placed ourselves in the chairs that were brought for us, said with a smile, that I was one of those who in the late session of the Scots parliament had opposed the interest of the court. My Lord, said I, does that character recommend met o Sir Ed— S—m-r? Sir, says Sir Ed—, it is to me a great recommendation of my Lord's good nature, to allow you to wait upon him: but it seems you are one who signalized yourself in the late session of your parliament, by framing Utopias and new models of government, under the name of limitations; in which you had the honour to be seconded and assisted by several men of quality, of about two or three and twenty years of age, whose long experience and consummate prudence in public affairs could not but produce wonderful schemes of government. This rough and sudden attack made me take the freedom to ask him, if he thought that men wanted any more than the knowledge and the will to govern themselves rightly. To which, continuing in his former strain, he answered, that young men were always ignorant, confident, and of insupportable arrogance. Yet, said I, do you not think that young men in parliament are much more capable to resist corruption, and oppose ill men, than they would be in a court, where by temptations arising from vanity and pleasure, they are in hazard of being corrupted themselves? Whereas in parliament meeting with no temptation but bribery, which that age abhors, or the ambition of getting a place by arts they are unacquainted with, the concern and assiduity of youth in their first applications is of great moment and highly useful, especially in men of quality, whose example and early virtue is of the greatest influence. And if with these qualifications they have also the talent of speaking well, it is not to be imagined how much their pleading for justice, with that sincerity and unaffected eloquence so natural to youth, does inflame the minds of men to all kind of virtue. You begin to declaim, as if they overheard you, said the old gentleman; but you must not think such stuff will have any influence upon me, or that I am so credulous to believe that boys of those years can have any right notion of government: an art which demands the longest experience and greatest practice. This kind of dialect I knew to be the usual way of Sir Edw-rd S--m-r, and therefore without the least show of resentment contented myself to say, that I was indeed of opinion, that to oppose the ill designs of inveterate knaves, is a work of great difficulty for young men to undertake; and that the common method of all governments now received in the world, to allow almost everything that tends to the corruption of manners, and then to restrain those corruptions, does not only require the longest experience and greatest prudence, but is far beyond the power of both. Yet to say that young men cannot understand the nature of government, and such regulations as are most conducing to the happiness of mankind, when at the same time they are thought capable of mathematics, natural philosophy, the art of reasoning, and metaphysical speculations, which contain things more difficult to conceive than any in the art of government, seems absurd. But by the present manner of education, the minds of young men are for many years debauched from all that duty and business to which they are born; and in the place of moral and civil knowledge and virtue, addict themselves to mathematical, natural, and metaphysical speculations, from which many are never able to withdraw their thoughts. For the interest of some governments requiring that men should know little of public affairs, the art of government has been looked upon as a kind of knowledge dangerous to be learned, except by those who are advanced in years; and this only so far as the experience and practice of those corrupt constitutions and ways of living now in use among men will allow. Whereas young men have great advantages to find out what is right or amiss in government, by having never been engaged in the ill administration of affairs, nor habituated to bad customs and indirect practices, nor biassed by selfish ends, to entertain any other opinion of constitutions, laws, and regulations, than what is just and right. And as their capacity for more abstracted sciences shows them sufficiently capable of understanding the art of government; and the innocence of their manners demonstrates that they are less biassed in judgment than other men; so in zeal and forwardness to put things in execution they are undoubtedly superior to all that are more advanced in years. The only difficulty in the education of youth is to fix their application on things useful. And do you not think the young men you mentioned very happy, who instead of studying physics and metaphysics, have employed their thoughts in an active way to advance the interest and service of their country? Their relations have taken care to marry most of them young, in order to prevent innumerable inconveniences; and if they enter into a good economy of their private fortunes, they may certainly acquire greater riches than they can hope to have a venture for at court. And if they despise the ridiculous vanity of great titles, which is the peculiar folly of this age, of what use and ornament may they not be to their friends and country, the care of which has possessed them so early? It is the experience of such men that will hereafter deserve to be valued, and not of those who from their youth have given themselves up to dissimulation and bad arts for worse ends, and are only skilled in the pernicious practices that tend to destroy the public liberty. Still declaiming! said he, and the result of all is, that there are not two more proper qualities for government, than want of experience, joined to the violent disposition of youth. But, said I, when these are corrected by the advice, and controlled by the votes of men of riper years, do you think them still dangerous?

I do.

Would they not be more dangerous, if the old men had only the power of advising, and that, for example, in the senate of a commonwealth all things were to be determined by the votes of the young men?

Certainly.

Would there not be yet greater danger, if the young men had the disposal of all places and advantages, and that the old men, in order to obtain them, should be obliged to flatter, and give such advice as they knew would please, and at the same time be pernicious to the state?

Who can doubt it?

Now if the young men, by reason of frequent disputes, heats, and factions among themselves, should choose one of their own number, and invest him with an unlimited power, though he were younger by many years than the gentlemen in question: I say, if any people should be so governed, would you not look upon it as a mad kind of government?

Most surely.

And yet many nations think they can be no way secure under any other sort of government than that which often falls into this very inconveniency. You mean, said he, a young prince in an absolute monarchy. Pray, said I, what think you of a young prince in a limited monarchy, not accountable to any? Do you doubt of instruments to execute his will, and of the confusion things may be brought to before redress can be obtained? Do you not think such a one equally dangerous to the state as the young men we have mentioned? Ay! but, said the knight, they bring faction into the state. I confess, said I, the young prince does not, because he is uncontrolled; so far you are right. But pray, Sir, what is it in those young noblemen, or in the proceedings of our parliament in general, that you think deserves so much blame? That they would talk, said he, of such limitations on a successor as tend to take away that dependence which your nation ought always to have upon us, as a much greater and more powerful people. I said, we are an independent nation, though very much declined in power and reputation since the union of the crowns, by neglecting to make such conditions with our kings, as were necessary to preserve both: that finding by experience the prejudice of this omission, we cannot be justly blamed for endeavouring to lay hold on the opportunity put into our hands, of enacting such conditions and limitations on a successor, upon the expiration of the present entail, as may secure the honour and sovereignty of our crown and kingdom, the freedom, frequency, and power of our parliaments, together with our religion, liberty, and trade, from either English or foreign influence. Sir Edw-rd all in a fret; hey day, said he, here is a fine cant indeed, independent nation! honour of our crown! and what not? Do you consider what proportion you bear to England? not one to forty in rents of land. Besides, our greatest riches arise from trade and manufactures, which you want. This was allowed by me: but I desired to inform him, that the trade of Scotland was considerable before the union of the crowns: that as the increase of the English trade had raised the value of their lands, so the loss of our trade had sunk the rents in Scotland, impoverished the tenant, and disabled him in most places from paying his landlord any otherwise than in corn; which practice has been attended with innumerable inconveniencies and great loss: that our trade was formerly in so flourishing a condition, that the shire of Fife alone had as many ships as now belong to the whole kingdom: that ten or twelve towns which lie on the south coast of that province, had at that time a very considerable trade, and in our days are little better than so many heaps of ruins: that our trade with France was very advantageous, by reason of the great privileges we enjoyed in that kingdom: that our commerce with Spain had been very considerable, and began during the wars between England and that nation; and that we drove a great trade in the Baltic with our fish, before the Dutch had wholly possessed themselves of that advantageous traffic. Upon the union of the crowns not only all this went to decay; but our money was spent in England, and not among ourselves; the furniture of our houses, and the best of our clothes and equipage was bought at London: and though particular persons of the Scots nation had many great and profitable places at court, to the high displeasure of the English, yet that was no advantage to our country, which was totally neglected, like a farm managed by servants, and not under the eye of the master. The great business both of Scots and English ministers was to extend the prerogative in Scotland, to the ruin of liberty, property, and trade: and the disorders which were afterwards occasioned by the civil war, gave the last and finishing blow to the riches and power of the nation. Since that time we have had neither spirit, nor liberty, nor trade, nor money among us. And though during the time of the usurper Cromwell we imagined ourselves to be in a tolerable condition with respect to this last particular, by reason of that expense which was made in the nation by those forces that kept us in subjection; yet this was a deceitful substance, not unlike a plumpness in the natural body proceeding from a disease. The business of a Scots minister is to get as much money as he can from our impoverished country, whilst he is in employment, well knowing that all regulations that may be established in order to enrich the nation, either by trade, manufactures, or husbandry, will require time before they can produce any considerable effect, and on that account will be of little advantage to him during his administration. I take all this freedom, said I, before the Earl of Cr-m-rty, though he be a Scots minister of state, because it is well known avarice is none of his faults, and that no person in our government is more ready to promote any new and solid project of improvement. I am obliged for the good character you give me, said the Earl; but very sorry I can promote none of your projects: they are I fear too great for our nation, and seem rather contrived to take place in a Platonic commonwealth than in the present corruption of things. My lord, said I, no man is more sensible how little is to be done in this age: but I think it the greatest of all follies to offer an expedient, which obtained will not answer the end, and to labour and toil for that which will not avail: such measures proceed in part from our ignorance of the ill condition we are in, and the means of recovery; but principally from a meanness of spirit, which hinders us always from applying the true remedies, if they are attended with the least appearance of difficulty or danger. And nothing does so much point out the want of sense and courage in particular men, or the degeneracy of an age and nation, than to content themselves to prosecute any considerable end by ineffectual and disproportionate means. Now the ill condition of Scotland proceeding from these causes; that our money is carried away and spent at court by those who attend there for places and pensions; that by the influence of English ministers upon our government, we are brought wholly to depend on that court; that by reason of the prince's absence, the laws are not put in execution: I say, these being the causes of our present ill condition, what other remedies can be found, than that the parliament of Scotland should for the time to come bestow all pensions and offices both civil and military; that our parliaments should be annual and not interrupted in their sessions, and have power to appoint committees for the administration of the government during the intervals of sitting? If these things are granted, said the Earl, I would know what power or authority is left to the prince. As great power, said I, as princes formerly enjoyed in most of the limited monarchies of Europe; their parliaments or diets were fixed, and at least annual: the chief officers of the crown and the counsellors of the prince were named by the states of most kingdoms; but the executive power of the government and the command of armies were vested in the prince, together with the prerogative of giving authority to the laws and currency to the coin, and a superiority in dignity and revenue, suitable to so high a station. But, said the Earl, you diminish his power of administration, not only by refusing him the nomination of great officers, but even the inferior: you encroach upon his power as general, by taking from him the nomination of military officers; and you lessen the grandeur of his court, by refusing him the distribution of pensions. To this charge I made answer, that if princes might not appoint the principal officers of the crown, nor their own counsellors, the nomination of inferior officers seems to be below their care and dignity; that standing forces being pernicious to all governments, and national militias only safe and useful, it is but reasonable the people should have the choice of those who are to command them; that his lordship could not forget that the limitations in question were demanded for a kingdom, where the prince does not actually reside, as a remedy against the influence of a powerful court, on which otherwise we should be necessitated always to depend. And I think for a nation in these circumstances to have the power of conferring pensions, can no way lessen the grandeur of a court, where no court is. The Earl said that no considerations whatever ought in such a degree to diminish the prince's power, which is the very essence of monarchical government; that no case could exist by which the essential part of any government could be so far lessened; and therefore such circumstances of affairs as I brought for reasons, being only accidents, could not be made use of to destroy the substance of a government. I told him I had always thought that princes were made for the good government of nations, and not the government of nations framed for the private advantage of princes. Right, said he, but then you must accommodate all monarchical government to the nature of princes, else you will make a heterogeneous body of the prince and state. I understand you not, said I, unless you mean that all limitations are contrary to the nature of princes, and that they will endure them no longer than necessity forces. And what hopes, said Sir Edw. S—r, can you have of enjoying them long, when your prince may be assisted by the power and riches of a far greater nation, which is highly concerned to take them away? I cannot think, replied I, that the people of England are obliged by their interest to oppose these limitations in Scotland, unless they think themselves concerned in interest to make us at all times their secret enemies, and ready to embrace every opportunity of declaring ourselves openly for such. For since we are not only become sensible of our present ill condition, but fully understand both the causes and the remedy; to oppose us in the prosecution of those means which are absolutely necessary to attain so just an end, would be no less than to declare open enmity against us. We shall run a great risk indeed, said Sir Edw-rd, in so doing! Sir, said I, no man is more fully persuaded than I am, of the great disproportion there is between the power of the one and the other nation, especially in the present way of making war. But you should consider, that by declaring yourselves in such a manner to be our enemies, you would drive us to the necessity of taking any power that will assist us, by the hand. And you can no way avoid so great danger, but by doing justice to yourselves and us, in not opposing any conditions we may make with the successor to our crown. The Earl of Cr-m-rty said, that in his opinion there was an easy remedy to all these inconveniencies;

which was a union of the two nations. I answered, I was sorry to differ so much from his lordship, as to think the union neither a thing easy to be effected, nor any project of that kind hitherto proposed, to be a remedy to our present bad condition: that the English nation had never since the union of the two crowns shown any great inclination to come to a nearer coalition with Scotland; and that I could not avoid making some remarks upon all the occasions that had given a rise to treat of this matter during my time. I have observed that a treaty of union has never been mentioned by the English, but with a design to amuse us when they apprehended any danger from our nation. And when their apprehensions were blown over, they have always shown they had no such intention. In the year 1669, endeavours were used in Scotland to establish a good militia; which on account of a clause procured by the duke of Lauderdale to be inserted in the act, in order to make his court, so alarmed the English nation, that in the following year a treaty of union was proposed. But so soon as they perceived that our militia was ordered in such a manner as neither to be lasting nor formidable, they presently cooled, and the union vanished. Upon the late revolution this treaty was again proposed: but when they saw we had chosen the same person for our king, and made the same entail of our crown they had done, the union, as a thing of no farther use to their affairs, was immediately dropped. For the same reasons, I suppose, the late treaty was set on foot; and after they had nominated a successor without asking our opinion or concurrence, they thought this the only way to amuse us, and oblige us to take the same person. Now as I have shown how little the English nation has been really inclined to the union, so I must acknowledge that the Scots, however fond they have formerly been of such a coalition, are now become much less concerned for the success of it, from a just sense they have that it would not only prove no remedy for our present ill condition, but increase the poverty of our country.

How, I pray? said the Earl.

I am of opinion, said I, that by an incorporating union, as they call it, of the two nations, Scotland will become more poor than ever.

Why so?

Because Scotsmen will then spend in England ten times more than now they do; which will soon exhaust the money of the nation. For besides the sums that members of parliament will every winter carry to London, all our countrymen who have plentiful estates will constantly reside there, no less than those of Ireland do at this time. No

Scotsman who expects any public employment will ever set his foot in Scotland; and every man that makes his fortune in England will purchase lands in that kingdom: our trade, which is the bait that covers the hook, will be only an inconsiderable retail, in a poor, remote, and barren country, where the richest of our nobility and gentry will no longer reside: and though we should allow all the visionary suppositions of those who are so fond of this union, yet our trade cannot possibly increase on a sudden. Whereas the expenses I mentioned will in a very short time exhaust us, and leave no stock for any kind of commerce. But, said the Earl, you do not distinguish right, nor consider where the fallacy of your reasoning lies. You talk of Scotland and Scots money, and do not reflect that we shall then be a part of Britain; England will be increased by the accession of Scotland, and both those names lost in that of Britain: so that you are to consider the good of that whole body, of which you then become a citizen, and will be much happier than you were, by being in all respects qualified to pretend to any office or employment in Britain, and may trade or purchase in any part of the island. But, by your leave, my lord, let me distinguish plainly, and tell you, that if I make a bargain for the people that inhabit the northern part of this island, I ought principally to consider the interest of those who shall continue to live in that place, that they may find their account in the agreement, and be better provided for than they are. For if the advantages of getting employments, trading, and purchasing in any part of the island are the only things to be considered, all these may be as well obtained by anyone who would change his country in the present state of things. And if in the union of several countries under one government, the prosperity and happiness of the different nations are not considered, as well as of the whole united body, those that are more remote from the seat of the government will be only made subservient to the interest of others, and their condition very miserable. On the other hand, besides our fishery, which God and nature has given us, together with the great privileges already granted to our African company, a distinct sovereignty does always enable a people to retain some riches, and leaves them without excuse if they do not rise to considerable wealth. So that if a sufficient provision be made to prevent the exhausting of our money by the attendance of Scotsmen at court, and to take away the influence of English ministers upon our affairs, no condition of men will be more happy. For we shall then be possessed of liberty; shall administer our own affairs, and be free from the corruptions of a court; we shall have the certain and constant alliance of a powerful nation, of the same language, religion, and government, lying between us and all enemies both by sea and land, and obliged in interest to keep perpetual peace and amity with us. And this you cannot but allow to be a much happier condition than any we ever could propose to ourselves by all the projects of union that have hitherto been formed. Here the Earl endeavoured by many arguments to show that our country would be the place, where all manufactures, as well for the use of the whole island, as for exportation, would be made by reason of the cheapness of living, and the many hands that Scotland could furnish. I said the contrary was not only most evident; but that the union would certainly destroy even those manufactures we now have. For example, the English are able to furnish us at an easier rate with better cloth than we make in Scotland: and it is not to be supposed they will destroy their own established manufactures to encourage ours. Corn and all manner of provisions are cheaper and more plentiful in the six northern counties than in Scotland. The number of our people was never so great as commonly imagined, and is now very much diminished by the late famine; by extraordinary levies of soldiers; and chiefly by ill government, which having given no encouragement to industry of any kind, has necessitated great numbers of men to abandon the country and settle themselves in other nations, especially in Ireland. Besides, the natural pride of our commonalty, and their indisposition to labour, are insuperable difficulties, which the English have not to contend with in their people. But sure you will allow, said the Earl, that a free commerce with England, and the liberty of trading to their plantations, which cannot be expected without a union, must be of incomparable advantage to the Scots nation, unless you will disown one of your darling clauses in the act of security. My lord, said I, the clause you mean is placed there without the condition of a union; and your lordship cannot forget, was brought in by the court as an equivalent for all limitations, and in order to throw out another clause, which declares that we would not nominate the same successor with England, unless sufficient limitations were first enacted. This was done to mislead the commissioners of burghs, who for the most part are for anything that bears the name of trade, though but a sham, as this was. And nothing could be more just than to turn it upon the court by adding both clauses; which sunk your party in the house for a long time after. For my own part, I cannot see what advantage a free trade to the English plantations would bring us, except a farther exhausting of our people, and the utter ruin of all our merchants, who should vainly pretend to carry that trade from the English. The Earl, who knew the truth of these things, was unwilling to insist any longer upon this ungrateful subject; and therefore proceeding to another argument, said that when we shall be united to England, trade and riches will circulate to the utmost part of the island; and that I could not be ignorant of the wealth which the remotest corners of the north and west of England possess. I answered, that the riches of those parts proceed from accidental causes. The lead and coal mines, which employ so much shipping, enrich the north. The western parts of England, besides mines of tin and lead, have many excellent harbours lying in the mouth of the Channel, through which the greatest trade of the world is continually passing. I desired him to consider that Wales, the only country that ever had united with England, lying at a less distance from London, and consequently more commodiously to participate in the circulation of a great trade than we do, after three or four hundred years, is still the only place of that kingdom, which has no considerable commerce, though possessed of one of the best ports in the whole island; a sufficient demonstration that trade is not a necessary consequence of a union with England. I added, that trade is now become the golden ball, for which all nations of the world are contending, and the occasion of so great partialities, that not only every nation is endeavouring to possess the trade of the whole world, but every city to draw all to itself; and that the English are no less guilty of these partialities than any other trading nation. At these words Sir Chr— was pleased to ask me what were those partialities in point of trade, of which the English were guilty, and towards what nations: that for his part, he accounted them the frankest dealers, and the justest traders of the world. I said I would not insist upon the ill usage of the Scots nation in their late attempt to settle in Darien, nor enquire how far the late erected council of trade did in that affair second the partialities of a court engaged in mysterious interests with France; but desired to know his opinion of the usage their own colony in Ireland had received from them, and that he would excuse me, if I should let fall any expression about that matter which might seem hard; because in case he could give me satisfaction in this particular, I should very much incline to an incorporating union of the two nations. He answered, that he was very indifferent what course the Scots should take in the matter of a union, yet would not refuse to argue the point with me; and as to my question concerning Ireland, he said, he was of opinion, that a good measure of strictness and severity is absolutely necessary to keep them from the thoughts of setting up for themselves, and pretending to depend no longer upon England. I said that some late writers had undertaken to prove by authentic records, that the relation of that country to England was founded rather upon a very strict union than a conquest. But certainly, though the native Irish were conquered, your own colony was not; which yet you favoured no longer than till you saw them begin to flourish and grow rich. And to show what we are to expect, if ever we begin to thrive, though never so long after our union, I shall give some instance of your conduct towards Ireland in relation to trade. A law was made that no tobacco should be planted either in England or Ireland; and another, that no person, except of England or Ireland, might trade to the English plantations. Yet in the time of King Charles the second, great hardships and impediments were laid upon all those who should trade from Ireland to the English plantations, though they were still obliged to observe the law against planting tobacco in Ireland. And till the time of the late King no law was made in England for encouraging the woollen manufacture, but the like encouragements were given to the people of Ireland. Yet during that reign a law was made, which prohibits the exportation of all woollen manufactures from Ireland to foreign parts, and lays so high a duty upon all that shall be imported from thence into England, as amounts to a prohibition. I forbear to mention any other hardships put upon those of that country, and chiefly the Scots who are settled in the northern parts, though that colony still increases, to our loss and your advantage. You speak of a conquered nation, said Sir Chr—, who have no sovereign rights belonging to them. I speak of a nation, said I, who affirm you have no shadow of right to make laws for them; that the power which the King's council has assumed was gotten by surprise; and that their first submission was founded on a treaty of union, which now on account of some rebellions suppressed, is called a conquest. But sure, as I said before, you never conquered your own colony, and therefore ought to do them justice. Now if after a union with us the least commotion should happen in Scotland, suppose on account of church government; might we not expect that the suppression of this would likewise be called a conquest, and we or our posterity be treated as a conquered people? But can there be a more certain indication of what we may expect in point of trade from a union, than the usage of the postnati, who settled in England and the plantations, upon the faith of rights declared and ratified by both houses of parliament, confirmed by the decisions of all your courts, and affirmed by the Lord chief Justice Coke in the most hyperbolical terms, to be according to common and all law, which yet have been wholly violated and taken away, even to the prejudice of the English nation by the loss of such a number of people? These things seem indispensably to require a guaranty, when the two parliaments come to be united, where we may possibly have fifty votes to five hundred, in a house already abounding so much in partialities, that the members who serve for one part of the kingdom are frequently found in opposition to the representatives of another, for the sake only of the particular interest of their own countries. Indeed, replied Sir Chr—, if your diffidence be so great, there can be no union. Sir, said I, if the matters of fact I mention are true, as I think they are undeniable, I am contented to make you judge of what we may expect from the nature of the thing, and genius of your people. In the first place, what security can a lesser nation, which unites to a greater, have, that all the conditions of union shall be duly observed, unless a third be admitted for guaranty of the agreement? And I suppose you would rather choose to hear no more of a union, than that Holland or France should be the guarantees. True, said he; but guarantees are only proper in treaties of peace between nations not united: unions of nations, especially incorporating unions, of which we are speaking, suppose no breach of conditions; and we do not find that the nations which were so united to the republic of Rome had any guarantees for their security. Sir, said I, the union of those nations, and their admission to the rights and privileges of the city of Rome, could have no guarantees, because they were noble conditions given by that wise and generous state to nations they had conquered, and had in their power to use as they pleased: and if Ireland be yours by conquest, why do you not use them as well? It will certainly be our interest, said Sir Chr—, to observe the conditions on which we unite with Scotland. Do you think, replied I, that you always follow your interest? I must acknowledge, said he, not always. Then, said I, if at any time you should depart from your true interest in this matter, we shall want a guarantee and find none. On the other hand, if the temper, conduct, and inclinations of your people be considered, it will appear that, except the union with Wales, which is still attended with great imperfections and inconveniencies, they have never shown the least disposition to unite with any other nation, though such as either stood upon equal terms with them, or such as they conquered, or even planted. How your colonies in America are treated is well known to all men. You never could unite with Normandy, which had conquered you, nor with any part of France that you had conquered. But your oppressions in both were the principal cause of your expulsion from those countries. You could not unite with the states of Holland, when England was likewise a republic. And since the time of the late revolution, which was effected by the assistance of the states, and saved these these nations from utter ruin, you can hardly endure the name of a Dutchman; and have treated them on all occasions with such scurrilous expressions, as are peculiar to the generality of your people. And if I should but touch upon the usage we continually meet with from this nation, I should not be believed, if all Europe were not sufficiently informed of their hatred to all strangers, and inveterate malice against the Scots. I know very well, that men of gravity and good breeding among you are not guilty of scurrilous reflections on any nation. But when we are to consider the case in question, we must have a just regard to the temper and general disposition of the people. At these words Sir Edw-rd, all in a flame, cries out, what a pother is here about a union with Scotland, of which all the advantage we shall have, will be no more than what a man gets by marrying a beggar, a louse for her portion? Upon this I turned to the Earl and Sir Chr—, and said, that if Sir Edw-rd had spoken these words in the House of Commons, I might not take notice of them, or question his freedom of speech in that place; but since he is pleased to express himself after this manner in a private conversation, I shall likewise take the liberty to say, that I wonder he is not afraid such language should make us suspect him not to be descended of the noble family whose name he bears. Sir Edw-rd going on with great passion: what account, said he, should we make of Scotland, so often trampled underfoot by our armies? Did not protector Seymour at the battle of Musselburgh give you such a rout as destroyed the best part of your nobility and gentry? And of late years did not the very scum of our nation conquer you? Yes, said I, after they had with our assistance conquered the King and the nobility and gentry of England: and yet that which you call a conquest was a dispute between parties, and not a national quarrel. It was, said he, inseparable from the fortune of our Edwards to triumph over your nation. Do you mean Edward of Carnarvon, said I, and his victory at Bannockburn? No, replied he, I mean Edward the first and third, whose heroic actions no princes have ever equalled. Sure, said I, you do not mean the honour of the first, or the humanity of the third so signally manifested at Berwick: nor the murder of Wallace by the first

Edward, or the poisoning of Randolph earl of Murray by the third, after they had both refused to give battle to those heroes. Sir Chr—, whose temper and gravity could not bear this upbraiding each other with old stories, interrupted these sallies, and desired I would farther explain myself touching a union between England and Ireland. The better conditions you give them, said I, the greater wisdom you will show. But you do not consider, said Sir Chr—, that Ireland lies more commodiously situated for trade, and has better harbours than England; and if they had the same freedom and privileges, might carry the trade from us. Ay, said I, there it is: trade is the constant stumbling block, and ball of contention. But do you think, that if Ireland, by a just and equal union with England, should increase in riches, such an increase would prove so prejudicial to England, where the seat of the government is?

Certainly.

Then, said I, it were better to exclude Ireland wholly from trade; for in that case the trade of England would increase by so much as Ireland now possesses; and the power and riches of England confined at home would be no longer in danger of passing into any other nation.

I believe you may be in the right.

You will certainly find me to be so, said I, if in order to manage this new accession of trade, all the people of Ireland should be brought over to England; for in this case the value of England would increase much more than can be expected to accrue from Ireland in the present circumstances of things, that country being frequently not only unprofitable but burdensome to England.

I agree with you.

But, said I, if Ireland should be left without inhabitants, I fear the French King would take hold of the occasion, and possess himself of the whole country. That would only weaken him, said he, who, grasping at the possession of the Spanish monarchy, has no number of people to spare. But, said I, a port in the province of Munster so near the entry of the Channel, and over-against Brest, might be of use to him, require no great number of men to maintain, and be of the most dangerous consequence to us. So that for argument sake we must suppose Ireland sunk in the sea; and then you will cease to fear either that they may set up for themselves, or carry away the trade from England. And being possessed of all their people and riches, you will be no longer liable to the expense of defending that kingdom. From these suppositions, said he, the consequence is just. Do you not think, continued I,

yet was possessed of many more than any of the provinces. I doubt not, said I, this order was very proper to retain the dominion of the world in the power of one city. But I think those nations might have lived more happily under another kind of regulation; and am fully persuaded, that all great governments, whether republics or monarchies, not only disturb the world in their rise and fall; but by bringing together such numbers of men and immense riches into one city, inevitably corrupt all good manners, and make them incapable of order and discipline, as you have already owned, and experience has but too well demonstrated. Rome, the greatest of all, incessantly disturbed her neighbours for seven hundred years; and after the conquest of almost all the known world, was corrupted by excess of riches and power, and spread the infection over all the parts of that empire, which at length brought in so many barbarous nations, and caused so many wars and so great effusion of blood, that the world suffered as much by the overthrow and destruction, as by the rise and continuance of that mighty power. Yet, said he, I think it is necessary that a considerable body of people should be united under one government, and by that means enabled to defend themselves against a powerful enemy, because by the successful ambition of some men, we frequently see great and formidable powers arise in the world, to the disturbance of all their neighbours. In that I perfectly agree with you, said I. Pray then, replied he, what numbers would you allow in such a body of men: or rather, what extent of territory would you think necessary to a right division of the world into several distinct governments, since you are so much an enemy to all great and overgrown powers? You seem willing, said I, to confer such an office upon me, that those who do not know my name will take me for a second Phaleg. Not to lay then too great a burden upon you at once, answered he, I desire you to acquaint us into what parts you would divide Europe, most commodiously to obtain the true ends of government. I replied, that God and nature seemed to have marked out certain portions of the world for several great societies of men; having divided them from each other by seas and mountains, or some remarkable difference of the soil and climate. The island of Britain and that of Ireland seem conveniently situated for one government: Spain and Portugal for another, because they lie together in one compact body, and are divided from the rest of Europe by the Pyrenean mountains. In like manner France is contained within the Alps, Jura, the Vosges, the Ardennes, and the Pyrenees. Italy is separated from all other parts by the Alps; and the three adjacent islands seem naturally to belong to that country. The seventeen Provinces, the circles of Westphalia and lower Saxony, with the archbishopric of Cologne and kingdom of Denmark, seem commodiously placed to be united under one government. The rest of Germany, with the Swiss Cantons and the provinces that lie between those countries and the Adriatic sea, might very well compose another. Norway, Sweden, Finland, Liefland, and the northern parts of European Muscovy, lying under the same climate, may be conveniently joined together. Poland, Prussia, Lithuania, and the southern parts of the European Muscovy, with the little Tartary, might likewise be properly united. The countries that lie to the north of Macedonia and Albania, and on the south of the Carpathian mountains, from Austria, Stiria, and Carniola to the Euxin sea, might be a ninth distinct government, and Macedonia, Albania, Thessaly, Epirus, Achaia, Morea, Negropont, Candia, and the adjacent islands, a tenth. And now I think I may rest, and take breath after so long a journey, leaving to any other the liberty of making the like through the other three parts of the world. What all this tends to I cannot imagine, said Sir Chr—, for by your division, our own government would continue to be of as great extent as now. You shall know that, said I, before we part. In the meantime, to justify in some measure the reasonableness of this division, you may consider that almost every one of the ten parts, into which I have divided Europe, speaks a language distinct from all the rest, and that the people are generally of the same temper and like dispositions. Sir Edw-rd, impatient to hear a discourse about so many things and places with which he is so little acquainted, thought fit to interrupt us; and directing his words to me: sir, said he, are you undertaking to teach us geography? Else what can you mean by such a division of Europe? Will you not allow, said I, a private man to make an imaginary division of countries; when it is well known that a great king in the beginning of the last age contrived one of the same nature? and you do not yet fully know what use I shall make of this division. You have led me into such a maze, said the Earl, and raised so many new thoughts in me, that without regard to our former reasoning, I must pursue some of them. That which occurs to me first, is, that if governments so equal in strength either on account of their riches or situation should come to be established, mankind might live in greater peace than they do: especially if these governments were by mutual alliances obliged to preserve the common tranquillity. But you are to observe, said Sir Chr—, the imperfection of this project to preserve peace in the world.

For though one or two of these governments might not dare to disturb and injure the rest, yet nothing can hinder one half of them from combining against the other. And as such wars would be managed by a far greater number of forces than the present, mankind must of consequence be made more miserable. The nature of human affairs is such, said I, that a perpetual peace is not to be preserved among men; yet certainly some constitutions of government are better fitted to maintain the public tranquillity than others. And in place of the continual great and ruinous wars, which questions about the succession of princes, and their ambitious designs, have entailed upon the world, things might be brought to less frequent contentions, and the public animosities either prevented from proceeding to open breaches; or if at some times wars could no way be avoided, they might be neither lasting nor bloody. If you can show, said he, how so happy a state of things may be introduced into the world, you will do the greatest service imaginable to mankind. For matters are now brought to such a pass, that in every war almost all Europe and America with a great part of Asia and Africa become engaged. You are in the right, said I; and these universal wars, as I may call them, which with little interruption have continued more than thirty years, have so distressed this part of the world, and occasioned such disorder in the affairs of men, that Europe is thought to be diminished a full fifth in value. For wars, besides that they are become universal, are now wholly managed by the force and power of money, and by that means most grievously oppress and afflict not only the places that are the theatres of action, but even the remotest village and most solitary cottage. And the French King having by the oppression of his subjects, and exact economy of his affairs, been able to keep such great numbers of troops on foot, has obliged the rest of Europe to a proportionable expense, and thereby made all wars by land at least twice as chargeable as formerly they were; and by sea to exceed all example. But to give you my opinion of this matter, I think mankind might be best preserved from such convulsions and misery, if instead of framing governments with regard only to a single society, as I believe all legislators have hitherto done, we should constitute such as would be no less advantageous to our neighbours than ourselves. You talk strangely, said Sir Chr—, as if our advantage were not frequently inconsistent with that of our neighbours. I am of opinion, replied I, that the true interest and good of any nation is the same with that of any other. I do not say that one society ought not to repel the injuries of another; but that no people ever did any injustice to a neighbouring nation, except by mistaking their own interest. You talk, said he, of injustice, but I speak of advantage. If you go about, said I, to take away by force any advantage that belongs to a neighbouring people, you not only do injustice to them, but injure yourself by the example. Whatever the example be, replied he, the advantage will accrue to my country. For the present, and in appearance, said I. But a citizen in the service of his country, said he, is not obliged to the same scruples as in his private affairs; and must be true to his public trust, and take care that the commonwealth suffer no prejudice. Then, said I, no man can be a good citizen of a particular commonwealth, and a citizen of the world; no man can be a true friend to his country and to mankind at the same time. I confess, said he, this conclusion naturally follows: but we may not dispense with the interest of our country as with our own; and you know the precepts contained in the sermon on the mount relate to the actions of private men. Do you think then, said I, that one nation cannot do injustice to another? Yes, answered he, when that which is done is to the prejudice of both. And do you not also think, said I, that one nation may make an unjust war against another?

Yes.

Then if your country should make such a war with success, they would have accomplished an unjust design. True, said he; but if thereby any advantage accrue to the nation, this becomes an acquired right to the people, and ought to be defended by all those who are intrusted with the public affairs. Now if afterwards it should happen, said I, that such a neighbouring nation should renew the war, in order to recover what they had lost, would that war be unjust on their part?

I think not.

Then you lay a foundation as well for your neighbours to make a just war against you, as for your own nation to make an advantageous war (which you say is not unjust) against them. This sure is far from the design of abolishing wars so far as may be possible. By what other means then, said he, may we hope to obtain this good end? The most effectual way, replied I, is, that all such governments as are of a sufficient force to defend themselves, should be rendered either incapable or unfit to make conquests. For the ambitious desires of men to increase their dominions have always been the principal cause of dis urbing the peace of the world. It is impossible, said Sir Edward S—m-r, to take away that natural and generous inclination which is found in the best of men, to extend the empire of their country;

especially among us, who have such great examples in our history to encourage us, and so noble and populous a city; which by being situated near the south-east point of the island, lies as conveniently to command the north of France and all the Low Countries, as the three kingdoms. But sir, said I, do you approve what Sir Chr— has said, that wars are to be abolished by all possible means? Suppose I do, said he; yet how can so strong an inclination, found not only in particular men, but sometimes in the whole body of a people, be altered? If the dominions of a state, said I, might not be increased by conquest.

How is that possible?

If, for example, said I, every one of those ten portions of Europe I mentioned before had ten or twelve sovereign cities well fortified within its territories, each of them possessing and governing the adjacent district: such a government strengthened with forts in passes, and other convenient places, might be very capable to defend itself, and yet altogether unfit for conquest.

Why so?

Because, said I, a conquest divided into twelve parts would be of little account, they could not be made adjacent to the several cities to which they ought to belong. But, said he, such conquered places might be governed in common to the advantage of the whole union. That, replied I, would be like a possession in common, for which no man has any particular affection, and on that account lies always neglected. But you talk, said Sir Edw—rd, of sovereign cities; I fancy you mean republics; which is nothing to us, who live under the benign influence of monarchy. You may suppose those cities, said I, to be the capitals of sovereign and independent kingdoms or countries. For of such sovereignties united under one monarch we have many examples. And the prince may either keep his court in each of them successively; or, which is better, reside in the country, and permit no more buildings about his palaces than are absolutely necessary for his domestics, and the dispatch of public business, and not to harbour a crew of lazy, profligate, and vicious wretches, fit only to render his court a mere sink of corruption, and a seminary to propagate all manner of vice through the whole nation. So that we may proceed to reason concerning the excellency of those governments, which consist of divers sovereignties united for their common defence, whether cities or kingdoms; whether independent already, or to be made so in order to put such a design in execution; whether governed by a prince, or by a great council of delegates. But certainly, said he, if these distinct sovereignties were incorporated under one head and city, such a government would be of greater force. If you mean, said I, to disturb their own peace, and that of their neighbours, I grant your assertion. How so?

You must acknowledge, said I, that a great city is more tumultuous and disorderly, and therefore more capable of disturbing its own peace than small ones, and much more violently inclined to conquer other countries, because better able to retain the conquest. But sure, said he, if divers small sovereignties were united under one prince, his authority would better preserve peace among them, than if they were governed by a council of delegates, which in my opinion is only proper to set them together by the ears. I am very glad, said I, that you think such united governments more suitable to monarchies than to common-wealths; for if that be true, there will be greater hopes of introducing them into the world. And indeed a prince seems much more fitted to be at the head of such a league, than a council, as to the military part, in which principally such a union has occasion to exert its power. So that I have nothing more to do than to prove that such governments are of all others the best to preserve mankind, as well from great and destructive wars, as from corruption of manners, and most proper to give to every part of the world that just share in the government of themselves which is due to them. If you can prove, said Sir Chr—, what you undertake, I shall have no more to say. It is indeed, said I, a most surprising thing to me, that not only all those who have ever actually formed governments, but even those who have written on that subject, and contrived schemes of constitutions, have, as I think, always framed them with respect only to particular nations, for whom they were designed, and without any regard to the rest of mankind. Since, as they could not but know that every society, as well as every private man, has a natural inclination to exceed in everything, and draw all advantages to itself, they might also have seen the necessity of curbing that exorbitant inclination, and obliging them to consider the general good and interest of mankind, on which that of every distinct society does in a great measure depend. And one would think that politicians, who ought to be the best of all moral philosophers, should have considered what a citizen of the world is. It is true, something like a consideration of the common good of mankind appeared in the constitution of the Achaian league; and if any of the ancients ever had a right view in this affair, the founders of that government

132

were the men. But the mighty power of the Roman commonwealth oppressed them in the very infancy of their establishment, and so deprived posterity of a perfect knowledge of the tendency of that constitution. Most governments have been framed for conquests; that is, to disturb the peace of mankind: though I know that some were less fitted for conquest than others, as the aristocratical. But there was nothing even in those constitutions that could sufficiently restrain the desire of enlarging their dominions, though no way formed to that end; which has frequently brought great calamities upon many of those governments, as the examples of Venice and Sparta demonstrate. In the last of which the wise legislator having formed the manners of the people for war, and the constitution altogether unfit to retain conquests, I would willingly persuade myself, that he designed these two things should balance each other, in order to keep that people always exercised to arms, and yet not give them the occasion of rising to such a height, as would inevitably precipitate them into ruin. And this, I think, should have been obvious to all legislators, that whoever contrives to make a people very rich and great, lays the foundation of their misery and destruction, which in a short time will necessarily overtake them. For such vicissitudes of human affairs are as certain as those of heat and cold in the revolution of the year; and no condiiton of men, or public societies, is durable and lasting, except such as are established in mediocrity. Now in small governments laws may be duly executed, and the manners of men in a great measure preserved from corruption: but because such governments are not of force sufficient to defend themselves, a considerable number of them should be united together for the common safety; by which union and league they will be enabled to resist a powerful invasion, and yet remain incapable of conquest. The three kingdoms of Scotland, England, and Ireland may serve for an example of this: which, though situated on islands, are yet in their present condition exposed to the fate of a single battle, if a great army of enemies could be landed near London. But if good forts were erected in the most considerable passes, and twelve cities with all the seaports well fortified, the loss of many battles would not determine the matter. And considering that our naval force might in a great measure intercept the supplies of the enemy, we might defend ourselves against all our neighbours. And as such a constitution would be altogether unfit to molest them, so it would give them little encouragement to disturb our peace. At this rate, said Sir Chr—, if we should continue long in peace, and unaccustomed to war, we might become a prey to the first invader. I answered, that I did not think we ought to be wholly unconcerned in the affairs of the Continent; but that such a constitution would certainly keep us from the danger of making conquests abroad, which in the present state of things any ambitious prince may attempt. Our militias might be usefully and honourably employed in assisting our neighbours to form the like leagues on the Continent; and a gradual propagation of such excellent governments would become easy, when mankind should be convinced of the great happiness and security they would enjoy by living under them. And though these leagues might possibly at some time make wars upon one another on occasion of a sudden pique, or to take revenge for some unneighbourly action; yet such wars could not be lasting, because nothing but hopes of making acquisitions and conquests can make them so. And as to the advantage of having twelve cities governing themselves happily and virtuously, instead of one great vicious and ungovernable city, I leave it to your consideration, who have so judiciously shown, that great cities do not only corrupt the manners of their own inhabitants, but those of whole nations, and destroy all good government. Cities of a moderate extent are easily governed, and the example and authority of one virtuous man is often sufficient to keep up good order and discipline; of which we have divers instances in the history of the Grecian republics: whereas great multitudes of men are always deaf to all remonstrances, and the frequency of ill example is more powerful than laws. But, said Sir Chr—, to reduce London within the compass of the old walls, seems a thing impracticable. This difficulty will be removed, replied I, when this city shall be only the capital of the neighbouring counties. It will be thought injustice, said he, to remove the seat of the government from a place which has been so long possessed of that great advantage. The injustice, said I, has been greater, that one place has so long enjoyed those profits which ought to have been divided among the considerable cities of the nation. I am afraid, said he, that all endeavours to disturb the affairs of so great a body of people, only out of a remote prospect of bettering their condition by a new regulation, may fall under the imputation of folly: and that men would think it hard to be plunged into such difficulties, as so great a change would necessarily occasion. Sir, said I, if a French King, when he is in peace with other nations, should suddenly attack us with his whole power, how can we resist him in our present condition; having no fortified cities, and the great seat of all our riches and power exposed to the very first insult of the invader?

One would think such a people were predestinated to ruin. You talk of the folly and hardship of putting men into some difficulties by a new regulation of their affairs, and seem not to consider how much more cruel a thing it would be to suffer these nations to be enslaved by a foreign invasion, or inevitably lose their liberty by that corruption of manners which this vicious and profligate city diffuses into every part. I did not foresee, said Sir Chr—, what use you would make of my complaint against the depravation of manners that reigns in this town, but acknowledge the consequence you draw to be just; and that if we design to diminish the corruption, we must lessen the city. What visions have we here? said Sir Edw-rd, destroy the greatest and most glorious city of the world to prosecute a whimsical project! Sir, replied I, you have heard what I have answered to Sir Chr—; and besides, do you not think the remoter parts of England injured by being obliged to have recourse to London for almost everything, and particularly for justice? Do you not think them wronged, in that almost all the treasure of England is yearly laid out in this place, and by that means the substance of the other parts exhausted, and their rents and revenues diminished? This, said he, is of little importance to the nation, so long as they continue to rise in the counties that lie nearest to the capital. I do not know that, replied I, but am of opinion, that if instead of one, we had twelve cities in these kingdoms possessed of equal advantages, so many centres of men, riches and power, would be much more advantageous than one. For this vast city is like the head of a rickety child, which by drawing to itself the nourishment that should be distributed in due proportions to the rest of the languishing body, becomes so over-charged, that frenzy and death unavoidably ensue. And if the number of people and their riches would be far greater in twelve cities than now in one, which I think no man will dispute; and that these cities were such as are situated in convenient distances from each other, the relief and advantages they would bring to every part of these kingdoms would be unspeakable. For example, if the people of York-shire or Devonshire were not obliged to go farther than York or Exeter to obtain justice, and consequently had no occasion to spend money out of those counties, how soon should we see another face of things in both? how soon would they double and treble their present value? That London should draw the riches and government of the three kingdoms to the south-east corner of this island is in some degree as unnatural as for one city to possess the riches and government of the world. And, as I said before, that men ought to be dispersed over all

135

countries in greater or lesser numbers according to the fertility of the soil; so no doubt justice should be administered to all in the most convenient manner that may be, and no man be obliged to seek it at an inconvenient distance. And if the other parts of government are not also communicated to every considerable body of men; but that some of them must be forced to depend upon others, and be governed by those who reside far from them, and little value any interest except their own, studying rather how to weaken them in order to make sure of their subjection; I say, all such governments are violent, unjust, and unnatural. I shall add, that so many different seats of government will highly encourage virtue. For all the same offices that belong to a great kingdom must be in each of them; with this difference, that the offices of such a kingdom being always burdened with more business than any one man can rightly execute, most things are abandoned to the rapacity of servants; and the extravagant profits of all great officers plunge them into all manner of luxury, and debauch them from doing good: whereas the offices of these lesser governments extending only over a moderate number of people, will be duly executed, and many men have occasions put into their hands of doing good to their fellow citizens. So many different seats of government will highly tend to the improvement of all arts and sciences; and afford great variety of entertainment to all foreigners and others of a curious and inquisitive genius, as the ancient cities of Greece did. I perceive now, said Sir Edw-rd, the tendency of all this discourse. On my conscience he has contrived the whole scheme to no other end than to set his own country on an equal foot with England and the rest of the world. To tell you the truth, said I, the insuperable difficulty I found of making my country happy by any other way, led me insensibly to the discovery of these things, which, if I mistake not, have no other tendency than to render, not only my own country, but all mankind as happy as the imperfections of human nature will admit. For I considered that in a state of separation from England, my country would be perpetually involved in bloody and destructive wars. And if we should be united to that kingdom in any other manner, we must of necessity fall under the miserable and languishing condition of all places that depend upon a remote seat of government. And pray where lies the prejudice, if the three kingdoms were united on so equal a foot, as for ever to take away all suspicion and jealousy of separation? that virtue and industry might be universally encouraged, and every part contribute cheerfully and in due proportion to the security and defence of this union, which will preserve us so effectually from those two great calamities, war and corruption of manners. This is the only just and rational kind of union. All other coalitions are but the unjust subjection of one people to another. Here I stopped; but after some pause finding the rest of the company silent, I continued to say, that I would not pretend to determine whether each of the portions into which I had divided Europe, should be confined to the precise number of twelve cities: though possibly if there were more, they might be subject to some confusion; and if not so many, would not answer the end: that I would not determine whether they should altogether consist of cities that are already considerable, as in these islands are London, Bristol, Exeter, Chester, Norwich, York, Stirling, Inverness, Dublin, Cork, Galway, Londonderry; or whether some other places more conveniently situated for strength, and more capable of fortification, might not rather be of the number. But this easy division of territory I think indispensably necessary, that to every city all the next adjacent country should belong. I was going on to open many things concerning these leagued governments, when a servant came to acquaint us that dinner was set on the table. We were nobly entertained, and after dinner I took leave of the company, and returned to my lodgings, having promised to meet them again at another time to discourse farther on the same subject.

My lords, I shall add nothing to this account, being persuaded that so long a narration has already sufficiently tired you.

I am,

Your most humble servant.

FINIS